Glencoe
WORLD HISTORY

Reproducible Lesson Plans

Glencoe McGraw-Hill

New York, New York   Columbus, Ohio   Chicago, Illinois   Peoria, Illinois   Woodland Hills, California

Glencoe/McGraw-Hill

A Division of The **McGraw·Hill** *Companies*

Send all inquiries to:
Glencoe/McGraw-Hill
8787 Orion Place
Columbus, Ohio 43240-4027

ISBN 0-07-829439-8

Printed in the United States of America

1 2 3 4 5 6 7 8 9 10   009 08 07 06 05 04 03 02

Contents

Chapter 17

Chapter 18

Chapter 19

Chapter 20

Chapter 21

Chapter 22

Chapter 23

Chapter 24

Chapter 25

To the Teacher

GUIDE TO USING THE REPRODUCIBLE LESSON PLANS

The *Reproducible Lesson Plans* are designed to help you organize your instruction, shorten your preparation time, and provide you with a variety of teaching options. Each Lesson Plan is organized so that you can easily identify the objectives, strategies, activities, and supplementary materials available (in the Teacher Wraparound Edition and Teacher Classroom Resources) for teaching that particular lesson. Each lesson plan also provides suggested ability levels for each activity listed (please see the key to ability levels below) and includes the expected range of completion time—or "presentation" time—for each activity (for example, 10–15 minutes). The Lesson Plans can be easily reproduced and submitted to your supervisor or administrator to fulfill your district's specific curriculum and preparation requirements.

For your convenience, a blank column is provided in which you may list objectives. The second block of each Lesson Plan begins with a list of the objectives that students should master after completing the section in the textbook. You may wish to point out these objectives to students and inform them that all review materials, as well as section quizzes and chapter and unit tests, will be designed to test their mastery of these objectives.

The five-step teaching model that follows the objectives in the Lesson Plans is designed to actively involve students as they learn about world history. These steps include:

FOCUS This section presents various activities available to you to introduce students to the section. It includes, for example, references to activities in the Teacher Wraparound Edition as well as to the appropriate Daily Focus Skills Transparencies located in the Teacher Classroom Resources.

TEACH The Teach section of each Lesson Plan is divided into two parts—Guided Practice and Independent Practice. The Guided Practice category directs you to activities in the side margins of the Teacher Wraparound Edition that are designed to be used with the entire class. In general, these are teacher-directed activities. The Guided Practice also directs you to other strategies included in the Teacher Wraparound Edition and the Teacher Classroom Resources.

The second category in the Teach section—Independent Practice—refers you to activities in which students take a more active role and assume more personal responsibility for mastering section objectives. These activities include the appropriate blackline masters in the Teacher Classroom Resources.

ASSESS The Assess section of each Lesson Plan is designed to help you measure student mastery of the section objectives. Within this portion, you are referred to the quizzes and tests—including online quizzes—that accompany the program. Alternately, you may wish students to use the Audio Program, the Interactive Tutor Self-Assessment CD-ROM, and/or the Reading Essentials and Study Guide available for each section.

RETEACHING AND ENRICHMENT The Reteaching and Enrichment section of each Lesson Plan refers you to the reteaching and enrichment activities in the Teacher Wraparound Edition as well as to the appropriate Reteaching Activity or Enrichment Activity in the Teacher Classroom Resources. In general, the reteaching activities are suitable for students who have not yet mastered the content of the section. The enrichment activities are designed to enrich and extend chapter content.

CLOSE The final section of each Lesson Plan—the Close section—refers you to the appropriate close activity in the Teacher Wraparound Edition.

KEY TO ABILITY LEVELS

Teaching strategies and student activities have been coded for varying learning styles and abilities:

L1 Basic activities for all students
L2 Average activities for average to above-average students
L3 Challenging activities for above-average students
ELL English Language Learner activities

Optional Resources Menu

Please use these additional activities and multimedia products for *Glencoe World History* to enhance your lessons and the study of world history.

TEACHER PLANNING AND SUPPORT RESOURCES

- TeacherWorks™ All-In-One Planner and Resource Center (Includes the Interactive Teacher Edition and Interactive Lesson Planner)
- Presentation Plus! CD-ROM
- Teaching Strategies for the World History Classroom (Including Block Scheduling Pacing Guides), TCR
- Inclusion for the High School Social Studies Classroom Strategies and Activities, TCR
- Daily Lecture and Discussion Notes, TCR
- *World History* Web site: wh.glencoe.com

REVIEW AND REINFORCEMENT RESOURCES

- Interactive Student Edition CD-ROM
- Glencoe Skillbuilder Interactive Workbook, Level 2 CD-ROM
- Cause-and-Effect Transparencies with Teaching Strategies and Student Activities, TCR

APPLICATION AND ENRICHMENT RESOURCES

- Social Studies Guide to Using the Internet, TCR
- World History Primary Source Document Library
- *World History* Video Program
- World Biography: People in History
- Reading in the Content Area

INTERDISCIPLINARY RESOURCES

- Team-Teaching Interdisciplinary Strategies and Activities, TCR
- World Art and Architecture Transparencies (with Strategies and Activities)
- World Art Prints (with Strategies and Activities)
- World Music: Cultural Traditions
- World Music: A Cultural Legacy
- Glencoe World Literature Library

MAP AND GEOGRAPHY RESOURCES

- Unit Map Overlay Transparencies with Strategies and Activities, TCR
- World Desk Map
- Building Geography Skills for Life
- Outline Map Resource Book

ASSESSMENT AND EVALUATION RESOURCES

- ExamView® Pro Testmaker CD-ROM
- Standardized Test Practice Workbook (and Teacher Annotated Edition), TCR

SPANISH RESOURCES

- Spanish Guided Reading Activities
- Spanish Reteaching Activities
- Spanish Quizzes and Tests
- Spanish Vocabulary Activities
- Spanish Summaries

Grade _____ Class(es) _____ Date _____ M Tu W Th F

Teacher's Name _____ Date _____

Early Humans

Section 1 *(pp. 19–25)*

LOCAL OBJECTIVES	TWE—Teacher Wraparound Edition TCR—Teacher Classroom Resources 📁 Blackline Master 📇 Transparency 💿 CD-ROM 🎧 Audio Program 📼 Videocassette 🖱️ Internet Resources

	OBJECTIVES **1.** By 10,000 B.C., *Homo sapiens sapiens* had spread throughout the world. **2.** Paleolithic peoples used technology.		

	FOCUS MENU	**SUGGESTED TIME RANGES**	**SUGGESTED LEVEL**
	—— Bellringer Skillbuilder Activity, TWE, p. 19; used with Daily Focus Skills Transparency or Blackline Master 1-1, TCR 📇 📁	5–10 minutes	L1
	—— Guide to Reading, TWE, p. 19	15–20 minutes	All levels
	—— Vocabulary Activity 1, TCR 📁	10–15 minutes	All levels
	—— Vocabulary PuzzleMaker 💿	15–20 minutes	All levels
	—— History Online Chapter 1 Overview 🖱️	10–15 minutes	L1
	TEACH MENU **Guided Practice**		
	—— Critical Thinking Activity, TWE, p. 20	15–20 minutes	L3
	—— Meeting Individual Needs, TWE, p. 21	5–10 minutes	L3
	—— Interdisciplinary Connections Activity, TWE, p. 22	20–25 minutes	L2
	—— Cooperative Learning Activity, TWE, p. 23	15–20 minutes	L1
	—— Critical Thinking, TWE, p. 24	5–10 minutes	L2
	—— Interdisciplinary Connections Activity, TWE, p. 24	10–15 minutes	L3
	—— Graphic Organizer Transparencies and Strategies 1, TCR 📇 📁	15–20 minutes	All levels
	—— Cooperative Learning Activity 1, TCR 📁	20–25 minutes	All levels
	Independent Practice		
	—— Guided Reading Activity 1-1, TCR 📁	15–20 minutes	L2, L3
	—— Skills Reinforcement Activity 1, TCR 📁	15–20 minutes	All levels
	—— Audio Program 🎧	30–35 minutes	All levels, ELL
	—— Primary Source Reading 1, TCR 📁	20–25 minutes	L2
	—— Historical Significance Activity 1, TCR 📁	10–15 minutes	L2
	ASSESS MENU **Evaluate**		
	—— Reading Essentials and Study Guide 1-1, TCR 📁	25–35 minutes	L1, ELL
	—— Section Quiz 1-1, TCR 📁	10–15 minutes	All levels
	—— Performance Assessment Activity 1, TCR 📁	15–20 minutes	All levels
	Reteach		
	—— Reteaching Activity, TWE, p. 25	10–15 minutes	L1
	Enrich		
	—— Enrich, TWE, p. 22	5–10 minutes	L1
	CLOSE MENU		
	—— Close, TWE, p. 25	10–15 minutes	L1

See Optional Resources menu on page viii.

The Neolithic Revolution and the Rise of Civilization

Section 2 (pp. 27–31)

LOCAL OBJECTIVES	TWE—Teacher Wraparound Edition 　　 TCR—Teacher Classroom Resources 　 Blackline Master 　 Transparency 　 CD-ROM 　 Audio Program 　 Videocassette 　 Internet Resources

OBJECTIVE

Systematic agriculture brought about major economic, political, and social changes for early humans.

FOCUS MENU	SUGGESTED TIME RANGES	SUGGESTED LEVEL
—— Bellringer Skillbuilder Activity, TWE, p. 27; used with Daily Focus Skills Transparency or Blackline Master 1-2, TCR	5–10 minutes	L1
—— Guide to Reading, TWE, p. 27	10–15 minutes	All levels
—— Vocabulary PuzzleMaker	15–20 minutes	All levels

TEACH MENU

Guided Practice

—— Critical Thinking, TWE, p. 29	10–15 minutes	L1
—— Meeting Individual Needs, TWE, p. 29	15–20 minutes	L1, ELL
—— History Online Student Web Activity 1		
—— Cooperative Learning Activity, TWE, p. 30	15–20 minutes	L2
—— Graphic Organizer Transparencies and Strategies 1, TCR	20–25 minutes	All levels
—— History Simulation 1, TCR	25–30 minutes	All levels

Independent Practice

—— Guided Reading Activity 1-2, TCR	15–20 minutes	L1, ELL
—— Audio Program	20–25 minutes	All levels, ELL
—— Time Line Activity 1, TCR	10–15 minutes	L1

ASSESS MENU

Evaluate

—— Reading Essentials and Study Guide 1-2, TCR	25–35 minutes	L1, ELL
—— Section Quiz 1-2, TCR	25–30 minutes	All levels
—— Chapter 1 Tests, TCR		
—— Interactive Tutor Self-Assessment CD-ROM, TCR	20–30 minutes	All levels
—— MindJogger Videoquiz, Chapter 1	20–25 minutes	All levels
—— History Online Self-Check Quiz 1	15–20 minutes	All levels

Reteach

—— Reteaching Activity, TWE, p. 31	5–10 minutes	L1
—— Reteaching Activity 1, TCR	15–20 minutes	L1

Enrich

—— Enrich, TWE, p. 29	15–20 minutes	L1
—— Enrichment Activity 1, TCR	15–20 minutes	L2

CLOSE MENU

—— Close, TWE, p. 31	15–20 minutes	L2

See Optional Resources menu on page viii.

Grade _____ Class(es) _____ Date _____ M Tu W Th F

Teacher's Name _____ Date _____

Civilization Begins in Mesopotamia   Section 1 *(pp. 37–43)*

LOCAL OBJECTIVES	TWE—Teacher Wraparound Edition TCR—Teacher Classroom Resources ▭ Blackline Master ✎ Transparency ⑨ CD-ROM ⓪ Audio Program ▣ Videocassette ➛ Internet Resources		
	OBJECTIVES **1.** Mesopotamia, one of the first civilizations, began between the Tigris and Euphrates Rivers. **2.** The Sumerians formed city-states and created forms of communication that affect our lives today.		
	FOCUS MENU	**SUGGESTED TIME RANGES**	**SUGGESTED LEVEL**
	—— Bellringer Skillbuilder Activity, TWE, p. 37; used with Daily Focus Skills Transparency or Blackline Master 2-1, TCR ✎ ▭	5–10 minutes	L1
	—— Guide to Reading, TWE, p. 37	15–20 minutes	All levels
	—— Vocabulary Activity 2, TCR ▭	10–15 minutes	All levels
	—— Vocabulary PuzzleMaker ⑨	15–20 minutes	All levels
	—— History Online Chapter 2 Overview ➛	10–15 minutes	L1
	TEACH MENU **Guided Practice**		
	—— Meeting Individual Needs, TWE, p. 38	5–10 minutes	L2
	—— Writing Activity, TWE, p. 39	10–15 minutes	L2
	—— Interdisciplinary Connections Activity, TWE, p. 40	20–25 minutes	L1
	—— Cooperative Learning Activity, TWE, p. 41	20–25 minutes	L1
	—— Writing Activity, TWE, p. 42	10–15 minutes	L2
	—— Critical Thinking Activity, TWE, p. 42	5–10 minutes	L2
	—— Graphic Organizer Transparencies and Strategies 2, TCR ✎ ▭	20–25 minutes	All levels
	Independent Practice		
	—— Guided Reading Activity 2-1, TCR ▭	15–20 minutes	All levels
	—— Audio Program ⓪	15–20 minutes	All levels
	—— Linking Past and Present Activity 2, TCR ▭	15–20 minutes	L2
	ASSESS MENU **Evaluate**		
	—— Reading Essentials and Study Guide 2-1, TCR ▭	25–35 minutes	L1, ELL
	—— Section Quiz 2-1, TCR ▭	10–15 minutes	All levels
	—— Interactive Tutor Self-Assessment CD-ROM, TCR ⑨	20–30 minutes	All levels
	—— MindJogger Videoquiz, Chapter 2 ▣	20–25 minutes	All levels
	Reteach —— Reteaching Activity, TWE, p. 43	5–10 minutes	L1
	Enrich —— Enrich, TWE, p. 38	5–10 minutes	L2
	CLOSE MENU —— Close, TWE, p. 43	20–25 minutes	L1

See Optional Resources menu on page viii.

Grade _____ Class(es) _____ Date _____ M Tu W Th F

Teacher's Name _____ Date _____

Egyptian Civilization: "The Gift of the Nile"

Section 2 *(pp. 45–53)*

LOCAL OBJECTIVES	TWE—Teacher Wraparound Edition TCR—Teacher Classroom Resources 🖿 Blackline Master 👆 Transparency 💿 CD-ROM 🔊 Audio Program 📼 Videocassette 🖱 Internet Resources

OBJECTIVES
1. The Nile was crucial to the development of Egyptian civilization.
2. Egyptian history is divided into three major periods.

		SUGGESTED TIME RANGES	SUGGESTED LEVEL
FOCUS MENU			
—— Bellringer Skillbuilder Activity, TWE, p. 45; used with Daily Focus Skills Transparency or Blackline Master 2-2, TCR 👆 🖿		5–10 minutes	L1
—— Guide to Reading, TWE, p. 45		15–20 minutes	All levels
—— Vocabulary PuzzleMaker 💿		15–20 minutes	All levels
TEACH MENU			
Guided Practice			
—— Charting Activity, TWE, p. 46		10–15 minutes	L1
—— Critical Thinking Activity, TWE, p. 46		10–15 minutes	L2
—— Meeting Individual Needs, TWE, p. 47		15–20 minutes	L1, ELL
—— History Online Student Web Activity 2 🖱			
—— Cooperative Learning Activity, TWE, p. 51		20–25 minutes	L3
—— Graphic Organizer Transparencies and Strategies 2, TCR 👆 🖿		20–25 minutes	All levels
—— Cooperative Learning Activity 2, TCR 🖿		20–25 minutes	All levels
Independent Practice			
—— Guided Reading Activity 2-2, TCR 🖿		15–20 minutes	L1, ELL
—— Audio Program 🔊		20–25 minutes	All levels, ELL
—— Time Line Activity 2, TCR 🖿		10–15 minutes	L1
—— Primary Source Reading 2, TCR 🖿		15–20 minutes	L1
—— Critical Thinking Skills Activity 2, TCR 🖿		10–15 minutes	L2
ASSESS MENU			
Evaluate			
—— Reading Essentials and Study Guide 2-2, TCR 🖿		25–35 minutes	L1, ELL
—— Section Quiz 2-2, TCR 🖿		10–15 minutes	All levels
—— Interactive Tutor Self-Assessment CD-ROM, TCR 💿		20–30 minutes	All levels
Reteach			
—— Reteaching Activity, TWE, p. 53		15–20 minutes	L1
Enrich			
—— Enrich, TWE, p. 48		5–10 minutes	L1
—— Enrich, TWE, p. 49		5–10 minutes	L2
—— Enrich, TWE, p. 52		5–10 minutes	L2
CLOSE MENU			
—— Close, TWE, p. 53		10–15 minutes	L3

See Optional Resources menu on page viii.

Grade _____ Class(es) _____ Date _____ M Tu W Th F

Teacher's Name _____ Date _____

New Centers of Civilization

Section 3 *(pp. 54–60)*

LOCAL OBJECTIVES	TWE—Teacher Wraparound Edition TCR—Teacher Classroom Resources 🗀 Blackline Master 🔖 Transparency 🅢 CD-ROM 🎧 Audio Program 📼 Videocassette ✒ Internet Resources

OBJECTIVES

1. The decline of the Hittites and Egyptians allowed a number of small kingdoms and city-states to emerge.

2. The Israelites did not create an empire, but they left a world religion, Judaism, that influenced the later religions of Christianity and Islam.

FOCUS MENU	**SUGGESTED TIME RANGES**	**SUGGESTED LEVEL**
—— Bellringer Skillbuilder Activity, TWE, p. 54; used with Daily Focus Skills Transparency or Blackline Master 2-3, TCR 🔖 🗀	5–10 minutes	L1
—— Guide to Reading, TWE, p. 54	5–10 minutes	All levels
—— Vocabulary PuzzleMaker 🅢	15–20 minutes	All levels

TEACH MENU

Guided Practice

—— Interdisciplinary Connections Activity, TWE, p. 55	15–20 minutes	ELL
—— Critical Thinking Activity, TWE, p. 56	10–15 minutes	L1, ELL
—— Meeting Individual Needs, TWE, p. 57	15–20 minutes	L1, ELL
—— Critical Thinking, TWE, p. 58	10–15 minutes	L2
—— Critical Thinking Activity, TWE, p. 59	10–15 minutes	L2
—— Graphic Organizer Transparencies and Strategies 2, TCR 🔖 🗀	20–25 minutes	All levels
—— History Simulation 2, TCR 🗀	30–35 minutes	All levels

Independent Practice

—— Guided Reading Activity 2-3, TCR 🗀	15–20 minutes	L1, ELL
—— Audio Program 🎧	20–25 minutes	All levels, ELL

ASSESS MENU

Evaluate

—— Reading Essentials and Study Guide 2-3, TCR 🗀	25–35 minutes	L1, ELL
—— Section Quiz 2-3, TCR 🗀	10–15 minutes	All levels
—— Interactive Tutor Self-Assessment CD-ROM, TCR 🅢	20–30 minutes	All levels

Reteach

—— Reteaching Activity, TWE, p. 60	10–15 minutes	L1

Enrich

—— Enrich, TWE, p. 56	15–20 minutes	L2
—— Enrich, TWE, p. 57	5–10 minutes	L1, ELL
—— Enrich, TWE, p. 60	10–15 minutes	L2
—— Enrichment Activity 2, TCR 🗀	15–20 minutes	L2

CLOSE MENU

—— Close, TWE, p. 60	5–10 minutes	L2

See Optional Resources menu on page viii.

The Rise of New Empires

Section 4 (pp. 61–64,

LOCAL OBJECTIVES	TWE—Teacher Wraparound Edition 📁 Blackline Master 🕯 Transparency 🎧 Audio Program 📼 Videocassette	TCR—Teacher Classroom Resources 💿 CD-ROM ⬤⁵ Internet Resources		
	OBJECTIVES **1.** The Hittites and Egyptians were eventually overshadowed by the rise of the Assyrian and Persian Empires. **2.** The Persian Empire brought many years of peace to Southwest Asia, increasing trade and the general well being of its peoples.			
	FOCUS MENU		**SUGGESTED TIME RANGES**	**SUGGESTED LEVEL**
	—— Bellringer Skillbuilder Activity, TWE, p. 61; used with Daily Focus Skills Transparency or Blackline Master 2-4, TCR 🕯 📁		5–10 minutes	L1
	—— Guide to Reading, TWE, p. 61		10–15 minutes	All levels
	—— Vocabulary PuzzleMaker 💿		15–20 minutes	All levels
	TEACH MENU **Guided Practice**			
	—— Interdisciplinary Connections Activity, TWE, p. 62		25–30 minutes	L2
	—— Critical Thinking Activity, TWE, p. 63		5–10 minutes	L1
	—— Graphic Organizer Transparencies and Strategies 2, TCR 🕯 📁		20–25 minutes	All levels
	Independent Practice			
	—— Guided Reading Activity 2-4, TCR 📁		15–20 minutes	L1, ELL
	—— Audio Program 🎧		20–25 minutes	All levels, ELL
	—— Skills Reinforcement Activity 2, TCR 📁		15–20 minutes	All levels
	ASSESS MENU **Evaluate**			
	—— Reading Essentials and Study Guide 2-4, TCR 📁		25–35 minutes	L1, ELL
	—— Section Quiz 2-4, TCR 📁		25–30 minutes	All levels
	—— Chapter 2 Tests, TCR 📁			
	—— Interactive Tutor Self-Assessment CD-ROM, TCR 💿		20–30 minutes	All levels
	—— MindJogger Videoquiz, Chapter 2 📼		20–25 minutes	All levels
	—— History Online Self-Check Quiz 2 ⬤⁵		15–20 minutes	All levels
	—— Performance Assessment Activity 2, TCR 📁		15–20 minutes	All levels
	Reteach			
	—— Reteaching Activity, TWE, p. 64		10–15 minutes	L1
	—— Reteaching Activity 2, TCR 📁		15–20 minutes	L1
	Enrich			
	—— Enrich, TWE, p. 63		10–15 minutes	L2
	CLOSE MENU —— Close, TWE, p. 64		5–10 minutes	L2

See Optional Resources menu on page viii.

Grade _____ Class(es) _____ Date _____ M Tu W Th F

Teacher's Name _____ Date _____

Early Civilization in India

Section 1 *(pp. 71–79)*

<table>
<tr><td rowspan="3">LOCAL OBJECTIVES</td><td colspan="3">TWE—Teacher Wraparound Edition   TCR—Teacher Classroom Resources</td></tr>
<tr><td colspan="3">📁 Blackline Master   🖳 Transparency   💿 CD-ROM</td></tr>
<tr><td colspan="3">🎧 Audio Program   📼 Videocassette   ➦ Internet Resources</td></tr>
<tr><td></td><td colspan="3">OBJECTIVES
1. India's earliest cities provided the foundation for the Aryans.
2. The caste system was a set of rigid social categories in Indian society.</td></tr>
<tr><td></td><td>FOCUS MENU</td><td>SUGGESTED TIME RANGES</td><td>SUGGESTED LEVEL</td></tr>
<tr><td></td><td>—— Bellringer Skillbuilder Activity, TWE, p. 71; used with Daily Focus Skills Transparency or Blackline Master 3-1, TCR 🖳 📁</td><td>5–10 minutes</td><td>L1</td></tr>
<tr><td></td><td>—— Guide to Reading, TWE, p. 71</td><td>15–20 minutes</td><td>All levels</td></tr>
<tr><td></td><td>—— Vocabulary Activity 3, TCR 📁</td><td>10–15 minutes</td><td>All levels</td></tr>
<tr><td></td><td>—— Vocabulary PuzzleMaker 💿</td><td>15–20 minutes</td><td>All levels</td></tr>
<tr><td></td><td>—— History Online Chapter 3 Overview ➦</td><td>10–15 minutes</td><td>L1</td></tr>
<tr><td></td><td>TEACH MENU
Guided Practice</td><td></td><td></td></tr>
<tr><td></td><td>—— Cooperative Learning Activity, TWE, p. 72</td><td>20–25 minutes</td><td>L2, ELL</td></tr>
<tr><td></td><td>—— Writing Activity, TWE, p. 73</td><td>10–15 minutes</td><td>L1, ELL</td></tr>
<tr><td></td><td>—— Meeting Individual Needs, TWE, p. 73</td><td>10–15 minutes</td><td>L2</td></tr>
<tr><td></td><td>—— Critical Thinking, TWE, p. 74</td><td>5–10 minutes</td><td>L1</td></tr>
<tr><td></td><td>—— Interdisciplinary Connections Activity, TWE, p. 74</td><td>5–10 minutes</td><td>L1</td></tr>
<tr><td></td><td>—— Writing Activity, TWE, p. 76</td><td>20–25 minutes</td><td>L2</td></tr>
<tr><td></td><td>—— Connecting Across Time, TWE, p. 78</td><td>5–10 minutes</td><td>L2</td></tr>
<tr><td></td><td>—— Critical Thinking Activity, TWE, p. 78</td><td>10–15 minutes</td><td>L2</td></tr>
<tr><td></td><td>—— History Online Student Web Activity 3 ➦</td><td></td><td></td></tr>
<tr><td></td><td>—— Graphic Organizer Transparencies and Strategies 3, TCR 🖳 📁</td><td>20–25 minutes</td><td>All levels</td></tr>
<tr><td></td><td>—— Cooperative Learning Activity 3, TCR 📁</td><td>20–25 minutes</td><td>All levels</td></tr>
<tr><td></td><td>Independent Practice</td><td></td><td></td></tr>
<tr><td></td><td>—— Guided Reading Activity 3-1, TCR 📁</td><td>15–20 minutes</td><td>All levels</td></tr>
<tr><td></td><td>—— Skills Reinforcement Activity 3, TCR 📁</td><td>15–20 minutes</td><td>All levels</td></tr>
<tr><td></td><td>—— Critical Thinking Skills Activity 3, TCR 📁</td><td>15–20 minutes</td><td>L1</td></tr>
<tr><td></td><td>ASSESS MENU
Evaluate</td><td></td><td></td></tr>
<tr><td></td><td>—— Reading Essentials and Study Guide 3-1, TCR 📁</td><td>25–35 minutes</td><td>L1, ELL</td></tr>
<tr><td></td><td>—— Section Quiz 3-1, TCR 📁</td><td>10–15 minutes</td><td>All levels</td></tr>
<tr><td></td><td>—— MindJogger Videoquiz, Chapter 3 📼</td><td>20–25 minutes</td><td>All levels</td></tr>
<tr><td></td><td>Reteach
—— Reteaching Activity, TWE, p. 79</td><td>5–10 minutes</td><td>L1</td></tr>
<tr><td></td><td>Enrich
—— Enrich, TWE, p. 75</td><td>10–15 minutes</td><td>L1, L2</td></tr>
<tr><td></td><td>CLOSE MENU
—— Close, TWE, p. 79</td><td>10–15 minutes</td><td>L1</td></tr>
</table>

See Optional Resources menu on page viii.

New Empires in India   Section 2 *(pp. 81–86)*

LOCAL OBJECTIVES	TWE—Teacher Wraparound Edition TCR—Teacher Classroom Resources 📁 Blackline Master 🖐 Transparency 💿 CD-ROM 🎧 Audio Program 📼 Videocassette 🔌 Internet Resources		
	OBJECTIVES **1.** The Mauryan dynasty flourished under Asoka. **2.** The Kushan kingdom prospered. **3.** The Gupta Empire left a lasting legacy through literature, architecture, and science.		
	FOCUS MENU	**SUGGESTED TIME RANGES**	**SUGGESTED LEVEL**
	—— Bellringer Skillbuilder Activity, TWE, p. 81; used with Daily Focus Skills Transparency or Blackline Master 3-2, TCR 🖐 📁	5–10 minutes	L1
	—— Guide to Reading, TWE, p. 81	15–20 minutes	All levels
	—— Vocabulary PuzzleMaker 💿	15–20 minutes	All levels
	TEACH MENU **Guided Practice**		
	—— Critical Thinking Activity, TWE, p. 82	20–25 minutes	L2
	—— Meeting Individual Needs, TWE, p. 83	10–15 minutes	L1, ELL
	—— Writing Activity, TWE, p. 84	15–20 minutes	L2
	—— Critical Thinking Activity, TWE, p. 85	20–25 minutes	L2
	—— Graphic Organizer Transparencies and Strategies 3, TCR 🖐 📁	20–25 minutes	All levels
	Independent Practice		
	—— Guided Reading Activity 3-2, TCR 📁	15–20 minutes	L1, ELL
	—— Audio Program 🎧	20–25 minutes	All levels, ELL
	—— Linking Past and Present Activity 3, TCR 📁	15–20 minutes	L2
	ASSESS MENU **Evaluate**		
	—— Reading Essentials and Study Guide 3-2, TCR 📁	25–35 minutes	L1, ELL
	—— Section Quiz 3-2, TCR 📁	10–15 minutes	All levels
	—— Interactive Tutor Self-Assessment CD-ROM, TCR 💿	20–30 minutes	All levels
	Reteach		
	—— Reteaching Activity, TWE, p. 86	5–10 minutes	L1
	Enrich		
	—— Enrich, TWE, p. 82	5–10 minutes	L2
	—— Enrich, TWE, p. 86	10–15 minutes	L2
	CLOSE MENU —— Close, TWE, p. 86	5–10 minutes	L2

See Optional Resources menu on page viii.

Grade _____ Class(es) _____ Date _____ M Tu W Th F

Teacher's Name _____ Date _____

Early Chinese Civilizations   Section 3 (pp. 88–97)

LOCAL OBJECTIVES	TWE—Teacher Wraparound Edition TCR—Teacher Classroom Resources 📁 Blackline Master 🖍 Transparency 💿 CD-ROM 🎧 Audio Program 📼 Videocassette 🖱 Internet Resources

	OBJECTIVES
	1. Chinese dynasties followed a rise and fall pattern.
	2. Three schools of thought about the nature of humans and the universe emerged.

	FOCUS MENU	**SUGGESTED TIME RANGES**	**SUGGESTED LEVEL**
	——— Bellringer Skillbuilder Activity, TWE, p. 88; used with Daily Focus Skills Transparency or Blackline Master 3-3, TCR 🖍 📁	5–10 minutes	L1
	——— Guide to Reading, TWE, p. 88	5–10 minutes	All levels
	——— Vocabulary PuzzleMaker 💿	15–20 minutes	All levels

	TEACH MENU		
	Guided Practice		
	——— Connecting Across Time, TWE, p. 90	5–10 minutes	L1
	——— Critical Thinking, TWE, p. 90	5–10 minutes	L1
	——— Interdisciplinary Connections Activity, TWE, p. 90	15–20 minutes	L3
	——— Connecting Across Time, TWE, p. 91	5–10 minutes	L2
	——— Writing Activity, TWE, p. 92	20–25 minutes	L1
	——— Critical Thinking Activity, TWE, p. 92	10–15 minutes	L2
	——— Critical Thinking Activity, TWE, p. 94	15–20 minutes	L3
	——— Critical Thinking, TWE, p. 95	5–10 minutes	L1
	——— Interdisciplinary Connections Activity, TWE, p. 95	20–25 minutes	L2
	——— Cooperative Learning Activity, TWE, p. 96	20–25 minutes	L1
	——— Graphic Organizer Transparencies and Strategies 3, TCR 🖍 📁	20–25 minutes	All levels
	Independent Practice		
	——— Guided Reading Activity 3-3, TCR 📁	15–20 minutes	L1, ELL
	——— Audio Program 🎧	20–25 minutes	All levels, ELL
	——— Primary Source Reading 3, TCR 📁	15–20 minutes	L2
	——— Historical Significance Activity 3, TCR 📁	15–20 minutes	L3

	ASSESS MENU		
	Evaluate		
	——— Reading Essentials and Study Guide 3-3, TCR 📁	25–35 minutes	L1, ELL
	——— Section Quiz 3-3, TCR 📁	10–15 minutes	All levels
	——— Interactive Tutor Self-Assessment CD-ROM, TCR 💿	20–30 minutes	All levels
	Reteach		
	——— Reteaching Activity, TWE, p. 97	10–15 minutes	L1
	Enrich		
	——— Enrich, TWE, p. 90	5–10 minutes	L2
	——— Enrichment Activity 3, TCR 📁	10–15 minutes	L1

	CLOSE MENU		
	——— Close, TWE, p. 97	15–20 minutes	L2

See Optional Resources menu on page viii.

REPRODUCIBLE LESSON PLAN **3–4**

Rise and Fall of Chinese Empires   Section 4 *(pp. 98–103)*

LOCAL OBJECTIVES	TWE—Teacher Wraparound Edition · Blackline Master · Transparency · Audio Program · Videocassette · TCR—Teacher Classroom Resources · CD-ROM · Internet Resources
	OBJECTIVES **1.** The Qin and Han dynasties established strong central governments that were the basis for future dynasties. **2.** Technical and cultural achievements during the Qin and Han dynasties included the inventions of paper and written literary classics.

	FOCUS MENU	SUGGESTED TIME RANGES	SUGGESTED LEVEL
	—— Bellringer Skillbuilder Activity, TWE, p. 98; used with Daily Focus Skills Transparency or Blackline Master 3-4, TCR	5–10 minutes	L1
	—— Guide to Reading, TWE, p. 98	10–15 minutes	All levels
	—— Vocabulary PuzzleMaker	15–20 minutes	All levels
	TEACH MENU **Guided Practice**		
	—— Meeting Individual Needs, TWE, p. 100	15–20 minutes	L2
	—— Writing Activity, TWE, p. 101	15–20 minutes	L1
	—— Connecting Across Time, TWE, p. 101	10–15 minutes	L2
	—— Charting Activity, TWE, p. 101	20–25 minutes	L1
	—— Cooperative Learning Activity, TWE, p. 101	30–35 minutes	L2
	—— Critical Thinking Activity, TWE, p. 102	10–15 minutes	L3
	—— Graphic Organizer Transparencies and Strategies 3, TCR	20–25 minutes	All levels
	—— History Simulation 3, TCR	25–30 minutes	All levels
	Independent Practice		
	—— Guided Reading Activity 3-4, TCR	15–20 minutes	L1, ELL
	—— Time Line Activity 3, TCR	10–15 minutes	L2
	ASSESS MENU **Evaluate**		
	—— Reading Essentials and Study Guide 3-4, TCR	25–35 minutes	L1, ELL
	—— Section Quiz 3-4, TCR	25–30 minutes	All levels
	—— Chapter 3 Tests, TCR		
	—— MindJogger Videoquiz, Chapter 3	20–25 minutes	All levels
	—— History Online Self-Check Quiz 3	15–20 minutes	All levels
	—— Performance Assessment Activity 3, TCR	20–25 minutes	All levels
	Reteach		
	—— Reteaching Activity, TWE, p. 103	10–15 minutes	L1, ELL
	—— Reteaching Activity 3, TCR	15–20 minutes	L1
	Enrich		
	—— Enrich, TWE, p. 100	10–15 minutes	L1, ELL
	CLOSE MENU —— Close, TWE, p. 103	15–20 minutes	L1

See Optional Resources menu on page viii.

Grade _____ Class(es) _____ Date _____ M Tu W Th F

Teacher's Name _____ Date _____

The First Greek Civilizations   Section 1 *(pp. 109–113)*

LOCAL OBJECTIVES	TWE—Teacher Wraparound Edition TCR—Teacher Classroom Resources 🗂 Blackline Master 🎙 Transparency 💿 CD-ROM 🎧 Audio Program 📼 Videocassette 🖱 Internet Resources
	OBJECTIVES **1.** Mycenaean civilization flourished in Greece between 1600 and 1100 B.C. **2.** The Greeks used the *Iliad* and *Odyssey* to present role models of the values of courage, honor, and excellence.

	FOCUS MENU	SUGGESTED TIME RANGES	SUGGESTED LEVEL
	—— Bellringer Skillbuilder Activity, TWE, p. 109; used with Daily Focus Skills Transparency or Blackline Master 4-1, TCR 🎙 🗂	5–10 minutes	L1
	—— Guide to Reading, TWE, p. 109	15–20 minutes	All levels
	—— Vocabulary Activity 4, TCR 🗂	10–15 minutes	All levels
	—— Vocabulary PuzzleMaker 💿	15–20 minutes	All levels
	—— History Online Chapter 4 Overview 🖱	10–15 minutes	L1

	TEACH MENU **Guided Practice**		
	—— Cooperative Learning Activity, TWE, p. 110	20–25 minutes	L1
	—— Writing Activity, TWE, p. 111	10–15 minutes	L2
	—— Critical Thinking Activity, TWE, p. 111	25–30 minutes	L3
	—— Interdisciplinary Connections Activity, TWE, p. 112	15–20 minutes	L2
	—— Graphic Organizer Transparencies and Strategies 4, TCR 🎙 🗂	20–25 minutes	All levels
	Independent Practice		
	—— Guided Reading Activity 4-1, TCR 🗂	15–20 minutes	All levels
	—— Skills Reinforcement Activity 4, TCR 🗂	15–20 minutes	All levels
	—— Audio Program 🎧	15–20 minutes	All levels

	ASSESS MENU **Evaluate**		
	—— Reading Essentials and Study Guide 4-1, TCR 🗂	25–35 minutes	L1, ELL
	—— Section Quiz 4-1, TCR 🗂	10–15 minutes	All levels
	—— Interactive Tutor Self-Assessment CD-ROM, TCR 💿	20–30 minutes	All levels
	—— MindJogger Videoquiz, Chapter 4 📼	20–25 minutes	All levels
	Reteach		
	—— Reteaching Activity, TWE, p. 113	5–10 minutes	L1
	Enrich		
	—— Enrich, TWE, p. 112	5–10 minutes	L1

	CLOSE MENU		
	—— Close, TWE, p. 113	5–10 minutes	L1

See Optional Resources menu on page viii.

The Greek City-States

Section 2 *(pp. 115–120)*

LOCAL OBJECTIVES	TWE—Teacher Wraparound Edition TCR—Teacher Classroom Resources
	📁 Blackline Master 🖊 Transparency 💿 CD-ROM
	🎧 Audio Program 📼 Videocassette 🖱 Internet Resources

	OBJECTIVES
	1. The polis or city-state was the central focus of Greek life.
	2. The search for farmland and the growth of trade resulted in colonies and the spread of Greek culture and politics.

	FOCUS MENU	**SUGGESTED TIME RANGES**	**SUGGESTED LEVEL**
	—— Bellringer Skillbuilder Activity, TWE, p. 115; used with Daily Focus Skills Transparency or Blackline Master 4-2, TCR 🖊 📁	5–10 minutes	L1
	—— Guide to Reading, TWE, p. 115	15–20 minutes	All levels
	—— Vocabulary PuzzleMaker 💿	15–20 minutes	All levels

	TEACH MENU		
	Guided Practice		
	—— Meeting Individual Needs, TWE, p. 116	15–20 minutes	L1
	—— Writing Activity, TWE, p. 117	15–20 minutes	L2
	—— Cooperative Learning Activity, TWE, p. 117	25–30 minutes	L1
	—— Writing Activity, TWE, p. 119	20–25 minutes	L2
	—— Graphic Organizer Transparencies and Strategies 4, TCR 🖊 📁	20–25 minutes	All levels
	Independent Practice		
	—— Guided Reading Activity 4-2, TCR 📁	15–20 minutes	L1, ELL
	—— Audio Program 🎧	20–25 minutes	All levels, ELL

	ASSESS MENU		
	Evaluate		
	—— Reading Essentials and Study Guide 4-2, TCR 📁	25–35 minutes	L1, ELL
	—— Section Quiz 4-2, TCR 📁	10–15 minutes	All levels
	—— Interactive Tutor Self-Assessment CD-ROM, TCR 💿	20–30 minutes	All levels
	Reteach		
	—— Reteaching Activity, TWE, p. 120	5–10 minutes	L1, ELL
	Enrich		
	—— Enrich, TWE, p. 118	10–15 minutes	L3

	CLOSE MENU		
	—— Close, TWE, p. 120	10–15 minutes	L2

See Optional Resources menu on page viii.

Classical Greece

Section 3 *(pp. 121–125)*

LOCAL OBJECTIVES	TWE—Teacher Wraparound Edition　　TCR—Teacher Classroom Resources 📁 Blackline Master　🖋 Transparency　💿 CD-ROM 🎧 Audio Program　📼 Videocassette　🖱 Internet Resources		
	OBJECTIVES **1.** During the Age of Pericles, Athens became the center of Greek culture. **2.** The creation of an Athenian empire led to war with Sparta.		
	FOCUS MENU	**SUGGESTED TIME RANGES**	**SUGGESTED LEVEL**
	—— Bellringer Skillbuilder Activity, TWE, 　　p. 121; used with Daily Focus Skills 　　Transparency or Blackline Master 4-3, TCR 🖋 📁	5–10 minutes	L1
	—— Guide to Reading, TWE, p. 121	5–10 minutes	All levels
	—— Vocabulary PuzzleMaker 💿	15–20 minutes	All levels
	TEACH MENU **Guided Practice**		
	—— Cooperative Learning Activity, TWE, p. 122	25–30 minutes	L2
	—— Turning Point, TWE, p. 123	10–15 minutes	L2
	—— Cooperative Learning Activity, TWE, p. 124	25–30 minutes	L1
	—— Connecting Across Time, TWE, p. 125	10–15 minutes	L3
	—— Graphic Organizer 　　Transparencies and Strategies 4, TCR 🖋 📁	20–25 minutes	All levels
	Independent Practice		
	—— Guided Reading Activity 4-3, TCR 📁	15–20 minutes	L1, ELL
	—— Audio Program 🎧	20–25 minutes	All levels, ELL
	—— Linking Past and Present Activity 4, TCR 📁	15–20 minutes	L2
	—— Historical Significance Activity 4, TCR 📁	20–25 minutes	L1
	—— Critical Thinking Skills Activity 4, TCR 📁	10–15 minutes	L1
	ASSESS MENU **Evaluate**		
	—— Reading Essentials and Study Guide 4-3, TCR 📁	25–35 minutes	L1, ELL
	—— Section Quiz 4-3, TCR 📁	10–15 minutes	All levels
	—— Interactive Tutor Self-Assessment CD-ROM, TCR 💿	20–30 minutes	All levels
	—— Performance Assessment Activity 4, TCR 📁	20–25 minutes	All levels
	Reteach —— Reteaching Activity, TWE, p. 125	5–10 minutes	L1, ELL
	Enrich —— Enrich, TWE, p. 123	10–15 minutes	L1
	CLOSE MENU —— Close, TWE, p. 125	5–10 minutes	L1

See Optional Resources menu on page viii.

The Culture of Classical Greece   Section 4 *(pp. 127–133)*

LOCAL OBJECTIVES	TWE—Teacher Wraparound Edition TCR—Teacher Classroom Resources 📁 Blackline Master 🔖 Transparency 💿 CD-ROM 🔊 Audio Program 📼 Videocassette 🖱 Internet Resources

	OBJECTIVES		
	1. Greek philosophers were connected with the development of critical or rational thought about the nature of the universe.		
	2. Greeks believed that ritualized religion was necessary for the well-being of the state.		

	FOCUS MENU	**SUGGESTED TIME RANGES**	**SUGGESTED LEVEL**
	—— Bellringer Skillbuilder Activity, TWE, p. 127; used with Daily Focus Skills Transparency or Blackline Master 4-4, TCR 🔖 📁	5–10 minutes	L1
	—— Guide to Reading, TWE, p. 127	5–10 minutes	All levels
	—— Vocabulary PuzzleMaker 💿	15–20 minutes	All levels

	TEACH MENU		
	Guided Practice		
	—— Interdisciplinary Connections Activity, TWE, p. 128	25–30 minutes	L2
	—— Meeting Individual Needs, TWE, p. 129	25–30 minutes	L1
	—— Writing Activity, TWE, p. 130	15–20 minutes	L2
	—— Connecting Across Time, TWE, p. 130	10–15 minutes	L2
	—— Interdisciplinary Connections Activity, TWE, p. 130	10–15 minutes	L2
	—— Critical Thinking, TWE, p. 131	10–15 minutes	L3
	—— Critical Thinking Activity, TWE, p. 131	20–25 minutes	L3
	—— Graphic Organizer Transparencies and Strategies 4, TCR 🔖 📁	20–25 minutes	All levels
	—— Cooperative Learning Activity 4, TCR 📁	20–25 minutes	All levels
	—— History Simulation 4, TCR 📁	30–35 minutes	All levels
	Independent Practice		
	—— Guided Reading Activity 4-4, TCR 📁	15–20 minutes	L1, ELL
	—— Audio Program 🔊	20–25 minutes	All levels, ELL
	—— Primary Source Reading 4, TCR 📁	20–25 minutes	L2

	ASSESS MENU		
	Evaluate		
	—— Reading Essentials and Study Guide 4-4, TCR 📁	25–35 minutes	L1, ELL
	—— Section Quiz 4-4, TCR 📁	10–15 minutes	All levels
	—— Interactive Tutor Self-Assessment CD-ROM, TCR 💿	20–30 minutes	All levels
	Reteach		
	—— Reteaching Activity, TWE, p. 133	10–15 minutes	L1
	Enrich		
	—— Enrich, TWE, p. 130	15–20 minutes	L1
	—— Enrich, TWE, p. 132	15–20 minutes	L2
	—— Enrichment Activity 4, TCR 📁	15–20 minutes	L2

	CLOSE MENU		
	—— Close, TWE, p. 133	5–10 minutes	L1

See Optional Resources menu on page viii.

Alexander and the Hellenistic Kingdoms

Section 5 *(pp. 138–143)*

LOCAL OBJECTIVES	TWE—Teacher Wraparound Edition 　　　TCR—Teacher Classroom Resources 📁 Blackline Master　🔦 Transparency　💿 CD-ROM 🎧 Audio Program　📼 Videocassette　🔗 Internet Resources		
	OBJECTIVES **1.** Under Alexander, Macedonians and Greeks conquered the Persian Empire. **2.** Hellenistic cities became centers for the spread of Greek culture.		
	FOCUS MENU	**SUGGESTED TIME RANGES**	**SUGGESTED LEVEL**
	—— Bellringer Skillbuilder Activity, TWE, p. 138; used with Daily Focus Skills Transparency or Blackline Master 4-5, TCR 🔦 📁	5–10 minutes	L1
	—— Guide to Reading, TWE, p. 138	10–15 minutes	All levels
	—— Vocabulary PuzzleMaker 💿	15–20 minutes	All levels
	TEACH MENU **Guided Practice**		
	—— History Online Student Web Activity 4 🔗		
	—— Writing Activity, TWE, p. 140	20–25 minutes	L3
	—— Cooperative Learning Activity, TWE, p. 140	30–35 minutes	L1
	—— Connecting Across Time, TWE, p. 141	5–10 minutes	L2
	—— Critical Thinking, TWE, p. 141	5–10 minutes	L1
	—— Interdisciplinary Connections Activity, TWE, p. 142	20–25 minutes	L3
	—— Connecting Across Time, TWE, p. 143	20–25 minutes	L2
	—— Graphic Organizer Transparencies and Strategies 4, TCR 🔦 📁	20–25 minutes	All levels
	Independent Practice		
	—— Guided Reading Activity 4-5, TCR 📁	15–20 minutes	L1, ELL
	—— Audio Program 🎧	20–25 minutes	All levels, ELL
	—— Time Line Activity 4, TCR 📁	10–15 minutes	L1
	ASSESS MENU **Evaluate**		
	—— Reading Essentials and Study Guide 4-5, TCR 📁	25–35 minutes	L1, ELL
	—— Section Quiz 4-5, TCR 📁	25–30 minutes	All levels
	—— Chapter 4 Tests, TCR 📁		
	—— Interactive Tutor Self-Assessment CD-ROM, TCR 💿	20–30 minutes	All levels
	—— MindJogger Videoquiz, Chapter 4 📼	20–25 minutes	All levels
	—— History Online Self-Check Quiz 4 🔗	15–20 minutes	All levels
	Reteach —— Reteaching Activity, TWE, p. 143	5–10 minutes	L1
	—— Reteaching Activity 4, TCR 📁	15–20 minutes	L1
	Enrich —— Enrich, TWE, p. 140	10–15 minutes	L3
	CLOSE MENU —— Close, TWE, p. 143	15–20 minutes	L1

See Optional Resources menu on page viii.

The Rise of Rome

Section 1 *(pp. 149–154)*

LOCAL OBJECTIVES	TWE—Teacher Wraparound Edition TCR—Teacher Classroom Resources 📁 Blackline Master ✋ Transparency 💿 CD-ROM 🎧 Audio Program 📼 Videocassette 🖱 Internet Resources

	OBJECTIVES
	1. The Romans conquered the plain of Latium, the Italian peninsula, and then the entire Mediterranean world.
	2. Their practical political skills allowed the Romans to maintain control over their conquered lands.

	FOCUS MENU	**SUGGESTED TIME RANGES**	**SUGGESTED LEVEL**
	—— Bellringer Skillbuilder Activity, TWE, p. 149; used with Daily Focus Skills Transparency or Blackline Master 5-1, TCR ✋ 📁	5–10 minutes	L1
	—— Guide to Reading, TWE, p. 149	15–20 minutes	All levels
	—— Vocabulary Activity 5, TCR 📁	10–15 minutes	All levels
	—— Vocabulary PuzzleMaker 💿	15–20 minutes	All levels
	—— History Online Chapter 5 Overview 🖱	10–15 minutes	L1

	TEACH MENU		
	Guided Practice		
	—— Cooperative Learning Activity, TWE, p. 150	20–25 minutes	L2
	—— Critical Thinking Activity, TWE, p. 151	15–20 minutes	L2
	—— Interdisciplinary Connections Activity, TWE, p. 152	25–30 minutes	L3
	—— Critical Thinking, TWE, p. 153	10–15 minutes	L2
	—— Meeting Individual Needs, TWE, p. 153	25–30 minutes	L2
	—— Graphic Organizer Transparencies and Strategies 5, TCR ✋ 📁	20–25 minutes	All levels
	Independent Practice		
	—— Guided Reading Activity 5-1, TCR 📁	15–20 minutes	All levels
	—— Audio Program 🎧	15–20 minutes	All levels

	ASSESS MENU		
	Evaluate		
	—— Reading Essentials and Study Guide 5-1, TCR 📁	25–35 minutes	L1, ELL
	—— Section Quiz 5-1, TCR 📁	10–15 minutes	All levels
	—— Interactive Tutor Self-Assessment CD-ROM, TCR 💿	20–30 minutes	All levels
	—— MindJogger Videoquiz, Chapter 5 📼	20–25 minutes	All levels
	Reteach		
	—— Reteaching Activity, TWE, p. 154	5–10 minutes	L1
	Enrich		
	—— Enrich, TWE, p. 152	20–25 minutes	L3

	CLOSE MENU		
	—— Close, TWE, p. 154	5–10 minutes	L1

See Optional Resources menu on page viii.

Grade _____ Class(es) _____ Date _____ M Tu W Th F

Teacher's Name _____ Date _____

From Republic to Empire   Section 2 *(pp. 156–162)*

LOCAL OBJECTIVES	TWE—Teacher Wraparound Edition TCR—Teacher Classroom Resources
	📁 Blackline Master ♨ Transparency 💿 CD-ROM
	🎧 Audio Program 📼 Videocassette 🖰 Internet Resources

	OBJECTIVES
	1. The internal instability of the Roman Empire eventually led to civil wars and increased power for the military.
	2. Octavian, titled Caesar Augustus, was named emperor, an event that stabilized the Roman Empire and paved the way for expansion and prosperity.

	FOCUS MENU	**SUGGESTED TIME RANGES**	**SUGGESTED LEVEL**
	—— Bellringer Skillbuilder Activity, TWE, p. 156; used with Daily Focus Skills Transparency or Blackline Master 5-2, TCR ♨ 📁	5–10 minutes	L1
	—— Guide to Reading, TWE, p. 156	15–20 minutes	All levels
	—— Vocabulary PuzzleMaker 💿	15–20 minutes	All levels

	TEACH MENU		
	Guided Practice		
	—— History Online Student Web Activity 5 🖰		
	—— Cooperative Learning Activity, TWE, p. 157	25–30 minutes	L3
	—— Meeting Individual Needs, TWE, p. 158	20–25 minutes	L1
	—— Connecting Across Time, TWE, p. 159	10–15 minutes	L2
	—— Critical Thinking Activity, TWE, p. 159	10–15 minutes	L2
	—— Connecting Across Time, TWE, p. 160	10–15 minutes	L3
	—— Interdisciplinary Connections Activity, TWE, p. 161	15–20 minutes	L2
	—— Connecting Across Time, TWE, p. 162	10–15 minutes	L1, ELL
	—— Graphic Organizer Transparencies and Strategies 5, TCR ♨ 📁	20–25 minutes	All levels
	Independent Practice		
	—— Guided Reading Activity 5-2, TCR 📁	15–20 minutes	L1, ELL
	—— Audio Program 🎧	20–25 minutes	All levels, ELL
	—— Critical Thinking Skills Activity 5, TCR 📁	10–15 minutes	L1

	ASSESS MENU		
	Evaluate		
	—— Reading Essentials and Study Guide 5-2, TCR 📁	25–35 minutes	L1, ELL
	—— Section Quiz 5-2, TCR 📁	10–15 minutes	All levels
	—— Interactive Tutor Self-Assessment CD-ROM, TCR 💿	20–30 minutes	All levels
	Reteach		
	—— Reteaching Activity, TWE, p. 161	5–10 minutes	L1
	Enrich		
	—— Enrich, TWE, p. 160	10–15 minutes	L3

	CLOSE MENU		
	—— Close, TWE, p. 162	10–15 minutes	L1

See Optional Resources menu on page viii.

Culture and Society in the Roman World

Section 3 *(pp. 163–168)*

LOCAL OBJECTIVES	TWE—Teacher Wraparound Edition TCR—Teacher Classroom Resources 📁 Blackline Master 🔦 Transparency 💿 CD-ROM 🎧 Audio Program 📼 Videocassette 🖱 Internet Resources

	OBJECTIVES **1.** Roman culture and society were heavily influenced by the Greeks. **2.** The Romans spread both Greek and Roman contributions to art, architecture, and literature throughout the empire.

	FOCUS MENU	**SUGGESTED TIME RANGES**	**SUGGESTED LEVEL**
	—— Bellringer Skillbuilder Activity, TWE, p. 163; used with Daily Focus Skills Transparency or Blackline Master 5-3, TCR 🔦 📁	5–10 minutes	L1
	—— Guide to Reading, TWE, p. 163	5–10 minutes	All levels
	—— Vocabulary PuzzleMaker 💿	15–20 minutes	All levels

	TEACH MENU **Guided Practice**		
	—— Interdisciplinary Connections Activity, TWE, p. 164	25–30 minutes	L2
	—— Cooperative Learning Activity, TWE, p. 165	20–25 minutes	L1
	—— Connecting Across Time, TWE, p. 166	5–10 minutes	L2
	—— Meeting Individual Needs, TWE, p. 166	15–20 minutes	L1
	—— Connecting Across Time, TWE, p. 167	15–20 minutes	L2
	—— Critical Thinking Activity, TWE, p. 167	20–25 minutes	L2
	—— Graphic Organizer Transparencies and Strategies 5, TCR 🔦 📁	20–25 minutes	All levels
	Independent Practice		
	—— Guided Reading Activity 5-3, TCR 📁	15–20 minutes	L1, ELL
	—— Audio Program 🎧	20–25 minutes	All levels, ELL
	—— Linking Past and Present Activity 5, TCR 📁	15–20 minutes	L2
	—— Historical Significance Activity 5, TCR 📁	10–15 minutes	L1

	ASSESS MENU **Evaluate**		
	—— Reading Essentials and Study Guide 5-3, TCR 📁	25–35 minutes	L1, ELL
	—— Section Quiz 5-3, TCR 📁	10–15 minutes	All levels
	—— Interactive Tutor Self-Assessment CD-ROM, TCR 💿	20–30 minutes	All levels
	Reteach		
	—— Reteaching Activity, TWE, p. 168	5–10 minutes	L1, ELL
	Enrich		
	—— Enrich, TWE, p. 166	15–20 minutes	L2

	CLOSE MENU		
	—— Close, TWE, p. 168	5–10 minutes	L1, ELL

See Optional Resources menu on page viii.

The Development of Christianity   Section 4 (pp. 169–174)

LOCAL OBJECTIVES	TWE—Teacher Wraparound Edition TCR—Teacher Classroom Resources 📁 Blackline Master ✍ Transparency 💿 CD-ROM 🎧 Audio Program 📼 Videocassette 🖱 Internet Resources

OBJECTIVES

1. Jesus, a Jew from Palestine, began his public preaching.

2. Christianity spread throughout the empire and eventually became the state religion of Rome.

FOCUS MENU	SUGGESTED TIME RANGES	SUGGESTED LEVEL
—— Bellringer Skillbuilder Activity, TWE, p. 169; used with Daily Focus Skills Transparency or Blackline Master 5-4, TCR ✍ 📁	5–10 minutes	L1
—— Guide to Reading, TWE, p. 169	5–10 minutes	All levels
—— Vocabulary PuzzleMaker 💿	15–20 minutes	All levels

TEACH MENU
Guided Practice

	SUGGESTED TIME RANGES	SUGGESTED LEVEL
—— Interdisciplinary Connections Activity, TWE, p. 170	10–15 minutes	L2
—— Writing Activity, TWE, p. 171	20–25 minutes	L1
—— Cooperative Learning Activity, TWE, p. 171	25–30 minutes	L2
—— Meeting Individual Needs, TWE, p. 172	25–30 minutes	L1
—— Critical Thinking Activity, TWE, p. 173	15–20 minutes	L2
—— Graphic Organizer Transparencies and Strategies 5, TCR ✍ 📁	20–25 minutes	All levels

Independent Practice

—— Guided Reading Activity 5-4, TCR 📁	15–20 minutes	L1, ELL
—— Audio Program 🎧	20–25 minutes	All levels, ELL

ASSESS MENU
Evaluate

—— Reading Essentials and Study Guide 5-4, TCR 📁	25–35 minutes	L1, ELL
—— Section Quiz 5-4, TCR 📁	10–15 minutes	All levels
—— Interactive Tutor Self-Assessment CD-ROM, TCR 💿	20–30 minutes	All levels

Reteach

—— Reteaching Activity, TWE, p. 173	10–15 minutes	L1, ELL

Enrich

—— Enrich, TWE, p. 174	20–25 minutes	L2

CLOSE MENU

—— Close, TWE, p. 174	15–20 minutes	L2

See Optional Resources menu on page viii.

Decline and Fall

Section 5 *(pp. 175–178)*

LOCAL OBJECTIVES	TWE—Teacher Wraparound Edition TCR—Teacher Classroom Resources
	📁 Blackline Master 🔖 Transparency 💿 CD-ROM 🎧 Audio Program 📼 Videocassette Internet Resources

	OBJECTIVES
	1. Under two strong emperors, Diocletian and Constantine, the Roman Empire gained a new lease on life.
	2. Ferocious warriors from Asia and Germany finally brought an end to the Roman Empire.

	FOCUS MENU	**SUGGESTED TIME RANGES**	**SUGGESTED LEVEL**
	—— Bellringer Skillbuilder Activity, TWE, p. 175; used with Daily Focus Skills Transparency or Blackline Master 5-5, TCR 🔖 📁	5–10 minutes	L1
	—— Guide to Reading, TWE, p. 175	10–15 minutes	All levels
	—— Vocabulary PuzzleMaker 💿	15–20 minutes	All levels

	TEACH MENU		
	Guided Practice		
	—— Critical Thinking Activity, TWE, p. 176	15–20 minutes	L3
	—— Graphic Organizer Transparencies and Strategies 5, TCR 🔖 📁	20–25 minutes	All levels
	—— Cooperative Learning Activity 5, TCR 📁	20–25 minutes	All levels
	—— History Simulation 5, TCR 📁	25–30 minutes	All levels
	Independent Practice		
	—— Guided Reading Activity 5-5, TCR 📁	15–20 minutes	L1, ELL
	—— Skills Reinforcement Activity 5, TCR 📁	15–20 minutes	All levels
	—— Audio Program 🎧	20–25 minutes	All levels, ELL
	—— Primary Source Reading 5, TCR 📁	20–25 minutes	L2
	—— Time Line Activity 5, TCR 📁	10–15 minutes	L1

	ASSESS MENU		
	Evaluate		
	—— Reading Essentials and Study Guide 5-5, TCR 📁	25–35 minutes	L1, ELL
	—— Section Quiz 5-5, TCR 📁	25–30 minutes	All levels
	—— Chapter 5 Tests, TCR 📁		
	—— Interactive Tutor Self-Assessment CD-ROM, TCR 💿	20–30 minutes	All levels
	—— MindJogger Videoquiz, Chapter 5 📼	20–25 minutes	All levels
	—— History Online Self-Check Quiz 5	15–20 minutes	All levels
	—— Performance Assessment Activity 5, TCR 📁	20–25 minutes	All levels
	Reteach		
	—— Reteaching Activity, TWE, p. 178	10–15 minutes	L2
	—— Reteaching Activity 5, TCR 📁	15–20 minutes	L1
	Enrich		
	—— Enrichment Activity 5, TCR 📁	15–20 minutes	L2

	CLOSE MENU		
	—— Close, TWE, p. 178	15–20 minutes	L1

See Optional Resources menu on page viii.

Grade _____ Class(es) _____ Date _____ M Tu W Th F

Teacher's Name _____ Date _____

The Rise of Islam

Section 1 *(pp. 191–194)*

LOCAL OBJECTIVES	TWE—Teacher Wraparound Edition TCR—Teacher Classroom Resources 📁 Blackline Master 🖋 Transparency ◎ CD-ROM 🎧 Audio Program 📼 Videocassette ⟿ Internet Resources

	OBJECTIVES **1.** In the fifth and sixth centuries, the Arabian Peninsula took on a new importance as a result of the caravan trade. **2.** The religion of Islam arose in the Arabian Peninsula and its prophet was a man named Muhammad.		
	FOCUS MENU	**SUGGESTED TIME RANGES**	**SUGGESTED LEVEL**
	—— Bellringer Skillbuilder Activity, TWE, p. 191; used with Daily Focus Skills Transparency or Blackline Master 6-1, TCR 🖋 📁	5–10 minutes	L1
	—— Guide to Reading, TWE, p. 191	15–20 minutes	All levels
	—— Vocabulary Activity 6, TCR 📁	10–15 minutes	All levels
	—— Vocabulary PuzzleMaker ◎	15–20 minutes	All levels
	—— History Online Chapter 6 Overview ⟿	10–15 minutes	L1
	TEACH MENU **Guided Practice**		
	—— Cooperative Learning Activity, TWE, p. 192	25–30 minutes	L2
	—— Critical Thinking Activity, TWE, p. 193	20–25 minutes	L2
	—— Graphic Organizer Transparencies and Strategies 6, TCR 🖋 📁	20–25 minutes	All levels
	Independent Practice		
	—— Guided Reading Activity 6-1, TCR 📁	15–20 minutes	All levels
	—— Audio Program 🎧	15–20 minutes	All levels
	—— Primary Source Reading 6, TCR 📁	20–25 minutes	L2
	—— Historical Significance Activity 6, TCR 📁	15–20 minutes	L2
	ASSESS MENU **Evaluate**		
	—— Reading Essentials and Study Guide 6-1, TCR 📁	25–35 minutes	L1, ELL
	—— Section Quiz 6-1, TCR 📁	10–15 minutes	All levels
	—— Interactive Tutor Self-Assessment CD-ROM, TCR ◎	20–30 minutes	All levels
	—— MindJogger Videoquiz, Chapter 6 📼	20–25 minutes	All levels
	—— Performance Assessment Activity 6, TCR 📁	15–20 minutes	All levels
	Reteach —— Reteaching Activity, TWE, p. 193	5–10 minutes	L1, ELL
	Enrich —— Enrichment Activity 6, TCR 📁	10–15 minutes	L1
	CLOSE MENU —— Close, TWE, p. 194	15–20 minutes	L2

See Optional Resources menu on page viii.

The Arab Empire and Its Successors   Section 2 *(pp. 196–202)*

LOCAL OBJECTIVES	TWE—Teacher Wraparound Edition · TCR—Teacher Classroom Resources · 📁 Blackline Master · 🖐 Transparency · 💿 CD-ROM · 🔊 Audio Program · 📼 Videocassette · 🖱 Internet Resources

OBJECTIVES

1. After Muhammad's death, his successor organized the Arabs and set in motion a great expansion.

2. Internal struggles weakened the empire and, by the close of the thirteenth century, the Arab Empire had ended.

FOCUS MENU	SUGGESTED TIME RANGES	SUGGESTED LEVEL
—— Bellringer Skillbuilder Activity, TWE, p. 196; used with Daily Focus Skills Transparency or Blackline Master 6-2, TCR 🖐 📁	5–10 minutes	L1
—— Guide to Reading, TWE, p. 196	15–20 minutes	All levels
—— Vocabulary PuzzleMaker 💿	15–20 minutes	All levels

TEACH MENU

Guided Practice

—— History Online Student Web Activity 6 🖱		
—— Critical Thinking Activity, TWE, p. 197	5–10 minutes	L2
—— Critical Thinking, TWE, p. 198	20–25 minutes	L1
—— Meeting Individual Needs, TWE, p. 198	25–30 minutes	L2
—— Connecting to the Past, TWE, p. 199	10–15 minutes	L1
—— Critical Thinking, TWE, p. 199	5–10 minutes	L2
—— Critical Thinking Activity, TWE, p. 199	20–25 minutes	L2
—— Connecting Across Time, TWE, p. 200	10–15 minutes	L2
—— Critical Thinking Activity, TWE, p. 200	15–20 minutes	L3
—— Critical Thinking Activity, TWE, p. 201	10–15 minutes	L3
—— Graphic Organizer Transparencies and Strategies 6, TCR 🖐 📁	20–25 minutes	All levels

Independent Practice

—— Guided Reading Activity 6-2, TCR 📁	15–20 minutes	L1, ELL
—— Audio Program 🔊	20–25 minutes	All levels, ELL

ASSESS MENU

Evaluate

—— Reading Essentials and Study Guide 6-2, TCR 📁	25–35 minutes	L1, ELL
—— Section Quiz 6-2, TCR 📁	10–15 minutes	All levels
—— Interactive Tutor Self-Assessment CD-ROM, TCR 💿	20–30 minutes	All levels

Reteach

—— Reteaching Activity, TWE, p. 202	5–10 minutes	L1

Enrich

—— Enrich, TWE, p. 200	15–20 minutes	L2

CLOSE MENU

—— Close, TWE, p. 202	10–15 minutes	L1

See Optional Resources menu on page viii.

Islamic Civilization

Section 3 *(pp. 203–206)*

LOCAL OBJECTIVES	TWE—Teacher Wraparound Edition TCR—Teacher Classroom Resources 📁 Blackline Master 🖨 Transparency 💿 CD-ROM 🎧 Audio Program 📼 Videocassette 🔗 Internet Resources

	OBJECTIVES **1.** An extensive trade network brought prosperity to the Islamic world. **2.** The Quran provided fundamental guidelines for all Muslims, not only in spiritual affairs but also in politics, economics, and social life.		
	FOCUS MENU	**SUGGESTED TIME RANGES**	**SUGGESTED LEVEL**
	—— Bellringer Skillbuilder Activity, TWE, p. 203; used with Daily Focus Skills Transparency or Blackline Master 6-3, TCR 🖨 📁	5–10 minutes	L1
	—— Guide to Reading, TWE, p. 203	5–10 minutes	All levels
	—— Vocabulary PuzzleMaker 💿	15–20 minutes	All levels
	TEACH MENU **Guided Practice**		
	—— Cooperative Learning Activity, TWE, p. 204	25–30 minutes	L2
	—— Critical Thinking Activity, TWE, p. 205	20–25 minutes	L2
	—— Graphic Organizer Transparencies and Strategies 6, TCR 🖨 📁	20–25 minutes	All levels
	Independent Practice		
	—— Guided Reading Activity 6-3, TCR 📁	15–20 minutes	L1, ELL
	—— Audio Program 🎧	20–25 minutes	All levels, ELL
	—— Critical Thinking Skills Activity 6, TCR 📁	10–15 minutes	L2
	ASSESS MENU **Evaluate**		
	—— Reading Essentials and Study Guide 6-3, TCR 📁	25–35 minutes	L1, ELL
	—— Section Quiz 6-3, TCR 📁	10–15 minutes	All levels
	—— Interactive Tutor Self-Assessment CD-ROM, TCR 💿	20–30 minutes	All levels
	Reteach		
	—— Reteaching Activity, TWE, p. 206	10–15 minutes	L1, ELL
	Enrich		
	—— Enrich, TWE, p. 205	25–30 minutes	L2
	CLOSE MENU		
	—— Close, TWE, p. 206	5–10 minutes	L1, ELL

See Optional Resources menu on page viii.

The Culture of Islam

Section 4 *(pp. 207–210)*

LOCAL OBJECTIVES	TWE—Teacher Wraparound Edition TCR—Teacher Classroom Resources 📁 Blackline Master 🖌 Transparency 💿 CD-ROM 🎧 Audio Program 📼 Videocassette 🖱 Internet Resources		
	OBJECTIVES **1.** Muslim scholars made great advances in the areas of mathematics and the natural sciences. **2.** Muslim art and architecture incorporated innovative, geometric styles of decoration.		
	FOCUS MENU	**SUGGESTED TIME RANGES**	**SUGGESTED LEVEL**
	—— Bellringer Skillbuilder Activity, TWE, p. 207; used with Daily Focus Skills Transparency or Blackline Master 6-4, TCR 🖌 📁	5–10 minutes	L1
	—— Guide to Reading, TWE, p. 207	10–15 minutes	All levels
	—— Vocabulary PuzzleMaker 💿	15–20 minutes	All levels
	TEACH MENU **Guided Practice**		
	—— Cooperative Learning Activity, TWE, p. 209	25–30 minutes	L3
	—— Graphic Organizer Transparencies and Strategies 6, TCR 🖌 📁	20–25 minutes	All levels
	—— Cooperative Learning Activity 6, TCR 📁	20–25 minutes	All levels
	—— History Simulation 6, TCR 📁	25–30 minutes	All levels
	Independent Practice		
	—— Guided Reading Activity 6-4, TCR 📁	15–20 minutes	L1, ELL
	—— Audio Program 🎧	20–25 minutes	All levels, ELL
	—— Skills Reinforcement Activity 6, TCR 📁	15–20 minutes	All levels
	—— Linking Past and Present Activity 6, TCR 📁	15–20 minutes	L1
	—— Time Line Activity 6, TCR 📁	10–15 minutes	L2
	ASSESS MENU **Evaluate**		
	—— Reading Essentials and Study Guide 6-4, TCR 📁	25–35 minutes	L1, ELL
	—— Section Quiz 6-4, TCR 📁	25–30 minutes	All levels
	—— Chapter 6 Tests, TCR 📁		
	—— Interactive Tutor Self-Assessment CD-ROM, TCR 💿	20–30 minutes	All levels
	—— MindJogger Videoquiz, Chapter 6 📼	20–25 minutes	All levels
	—— History Online Self-Check Quiz 6 🖱	15–20 minutes	All levels
	Reteach		
	—— Reteaching Activity, TWE, p. 210	10–15 minutes	L1, ELL
	—— Reteaching Activity 6, TCR 📁	15–20 minutes	L1
	CLOSE MENU		
	—— Close, TWE, p. 210	10–15 minutes	L2

See Optional Resources menu on page viii.

The Development of Civilizations in Africa

Section 1 *(pp. 223–226)*

LOCAL OBJECTIVES	TWE—Teacher Wraparound Edition TCR—Teacher Classroom Resources 📁 Blackline Master 🖋 Transparency 💿 CD-ROM 🎧 Audio Program 📼 Videocassette 🖱 Internet Resources

	OBJECTIVES
	1. Africa's four distinct climate zones affected the development of African civilizations. **2.** The mastery of farming gave rise to the first civilizations in Africa: Egypt, Kush, and Axum.

	FOCUS MENU	**SUGGESTED TIME RANGES**	**SUGGESTED LEVEL**
	—— Bellringer Skillbuilder Activity, TWE, p. 223; used with Daily Focus Skills Transparency or Blackline Master 7-1, TCR 🖋 📁	5–10 minutes	L1
	—— Guide to Reading, TWE, p. 223	15–20 minutes	All levels
	—— Vocabulary Activity 7, TCR 📁	10–15 minutes	All levels
	—— Vocabulary PuzzleMaker 💿	15–20 minutes	All levels
	—— History Online Chapter 7 Overview 🖱	10–15 minutes	L1

	TEACH MENU		
	Guided Practice		
	—— Interdisciplinary Connections Activity, TWE, p. 224	20–25 minutes	L2
	—— Cooperative Learning Activity, TWE, p. 225	25–30 minutes	L2
	—— Graphic Organizer Transparencies and Strategies 7, TCR 🖋 📁	20–25 minutes	All levels
	—— Cooperative Learning Activity 7, TCR 📁	20–25 minutes	All levels
	Independent Practice		
	—— Guided Reading Activity 7-1, TCR 📁	15–20 minutes	All levels
	—— Skills Reinforcement Activity 7, TCR 📁	15–20 minutes	All levels
	—— Audio Program 🎧	15–20 minutes	All levels

	ASSESS MENU		
	Evaluate		
	—— Reading Essentials and Study Guide 7-1, TCR 📁	25–35 minutes	L1, ELL
	—— Section Quiz 7-1, TCR 📁	10–15 minutes	All levels
	—— Interactive Tutor Self-Assessment CD-ROM, TCR 💿	20–30 minutes	All levels
	—— MindJogger Videoquiz, Chapter 7 📼	20–25 minutes	All levels
	Reteach		
	—— Reteaching Activity, TWE, p. 226	5–10 minutes	L1

	CLOSE MENU		
	—— Close, TWE, p. 226	10–15 minutes	L1

See Optional Resources menu on page viii.

Kingdoms and States of Africa   Section 2 *(pp. 228–235)*

LOCAL OBJECTIVES	TWE—Teacher Wraparound Edition TCR—Teacher Classroom Resources 📁 Blackline Master ✋ Transparency 🔘 CD-ROM 🎧 Audio Program 📼 Videocassette 🖱 Internet Resources
	OBJECTIVES **1.** The expansion of trade led to migration and the growth of new kingdoms. **2.** Rulers introduced different forms of government.

	FOCUS MENU	SUGGESTED TIME RANGES	SUGGESTED LEVEL
	—— Bellringer Skillbuilder Activity, TWE, p. 228; used with Daily Focus Skills Transparency or Blackline Master 7-2, TCR ✋ 📁	5–10 minutes	L1
	—— Guide to Reading, TWE, p. 228	15–20 minutes	All levels
	—— Vocabulary PuzzleMaker 🔘	15–20 minutes	All levels

	TEACH MENU		
	Guided Practice		
	—— Meeting Individual Needs, TWE, p. 229	15–20 minutes	L1, ELL
	—— Cooperative Learning Activity, TWE, p. 231	25–30 minutes	L2
	—— Charting Activity, TWE, p. 232	15–20 minutes	L1
	—— Graphic Organizer Transparencies and Strategies 7, TCR ✋ 📁	20–25 minutes	All levels
	Independent Practice		
	—— Guided Reading Activity 7-2, TCR 📁	15–20 minutes	L1, ELL
	—— Audio Program 🎧	20–25 minutes	All levels, ELL
	—— Linking Past and Present Activity 7, TCR 📁	15–20 minutes	L2
	—— Primary Source Reading 7, TCR 📁	20–25 minutes	L3
	—— Historical Significance Activity 7, TCR 📁	15–20 minutes	L1
	—— Time Line Activity 7, TCR 📁	10–15 minutes	L1

	ASSESS MENU		
	Evaluate		
	—— Reading Essentials and Study Guide 7-2, TCR 📁	25–35 minutes	L1, ELL
	—— Section Quiz 7-2, TCR 📁	10–15 minutes	All levels
	—— Interactive Tutor Self-Assessment CD-ROM, TCR 🔘	20–30 minutes	All levels
	Reteach		
	—— Reteaching Activity, TWE, p. 234	10–15 minutes	L1
	Enrich		
	—— Enrich, TWE, p. 230	10–15 minutes	L1

	CLOSE MENU		
	—— Close, TWE, p. 234	5–10 minutes	L1

See Optional Resources menu on page viii.

Grade _____ Class(es) _____ Date _____ M Tu W Th F

Teacher's Name _____ Date _____

African Society and Culture   Section 3 (pp. 236–241)

LOCAL OBJECTIVES	TWE—Teacher Wraparound Edition TCR—Teacher Classroom Resources 📁 Blackline Master ✍ Transparency 💿 CD-ROM 🎧 Audio Program 📼 Videocassette 🔗 Internet Resources		
	OBJECTIVES **1.** Extended family units formed the basis of African villages. **2.** The arts were important in early African culture.		
	FOCUS MENU	**SUGGESTED TIME RANGES**	**SUGGESTED LEVEL**
	——— Bellringer Skillbuilder Activity, TWE, p. 236; used with Daily Focus Skills Transparency or Blackline Master 7-3, TCR ✍ 📁	5–10 minutes	L1
	——— Guide to Reading, TWE, p. 236	10–15 minutes	All levels
	——— Vocabulary PuzzleMaker 💿	15–20 minutes	All levels
	TEACH MENU **Guided Practice**		
	——— Writing Activity, TWE, p. 238	15–20 minutes	L2
	——— Connecting Across Time, TWE, p. 238	5–10 minutes	L2
	——— Critical Thinking Activity, TWE, p. 238	5–10 minutes	L3
	——— History Online Student Web Activity 7 🔗		
	——— Cooperative Learning Activity, TWE, p. 239	25–30 minutes	L2, ELL
	——— Interdisciplinary Connections Activity, TWE, p. 240	15–20 minutes	L3
	——— Graphic Organizer Transparencies and Strategies 7, TCR ✍ 📁	20–25 minutes	All levels
	——— History Simulation 7, TCR 📁	25–30 minutes	All levels
	Independent Practice		
	——— Guided Reading Activity 7-3, TCR 📁	15–20 minutes	L1, ELL
	——— Audio Program 🎧	20–25 minutes	All levels, ELL
	——— Critical Thinking Skills Activity 7, TCR 📁	10–15 minutes	L2
	ASSESS MENU **Evaluate**		
	——— Reading Essentials and Study Guide 7-3, TCR 📁	25–35 minutes	L1, ELL
	——— Section Quiz 7-3, TCR 📁	25–30 minutes	All levels
	——— Chapter 7 Tests, TCR 📁		
	——— Interactive Tutor Self-Assessment CD-ROM, TCR 💿	20–30 minutes	All levels
	——— MindJogger Videoquiz, Chapter 7 📼	20–25 minutes	All levels
	——— History Online Self-Check Quiz 7 🔗	15–20 minutes	All levels
	——— Performance Assessment Activity 7, TCR 📁	20–25 minutes	All levels
	Reteach		
	——— Reteaching Activity, TWE, p. 241	5–10 minutes	L2
	——— Reteaching Activity 7, TCR 📁	15–20 minutes	L1
	Enrich		
	——— Enrichment Activity 7, TCR 📁	20–25 minutes	L3
	CLOSE MENU		
	——— Close, TWE, p. 241	5–10 minutes	L1

See Optional Resources menu on page viii.

China Reunified
Section 1 *(pp. 247–252)*

LOCAL OBJECTIVES	TWE—Teacher Wraparound Edition TCR—Teacher Classroom Resources
	📁 Blackline Master 🖨 Transparency 💿 CD-ROM
	🎧 Audio Program 📼 Videocassette 🖱 Internet Resources

OBJECTIVES

1. The Sui, Tang, and Song dynasties restored peace to China in between periods of chaos and disorder.

2. Innovations and reforms in government, agriculture, and technology brought periods of growth and prosperity to China.

FOCUS MENU	SUGGESTED TIME RANGES	SUGGESTED LEVEL
—— Bellringer Skillbuilder Activity, TWE, p. 247; used with Daily Focus Skills Transparency or Blackline Master 8-1, TCR 🖨 📁	5–10 minutes	L1
—— Guide to Reading, TWE, p. 247	15–20 minutes	All levels
—— Vocabulary Activity 8, TCR 📁	10–15 minutes	All levels
—— Vocabulary PuzzleMaker 💿	15–20 minutes	All levels
—— History Online Chapter 8 Overview 🖱	10–15 minutes	L1

TEACH MENU

Guided Practice

—— Critical Thinking Activity, TWE, p. 248	10–15 minutes	L1
—— Cooperative Learning Activity, TWE, p. 248	20–25 minutes	L2
—— Critical Thinking Activity, TWE, p. 249	10–15 minutes	L2
—— Connecting Across Time, TWE, p. 250	25–30 minutes	L2
—— Critical Thinking Activity, TWE, p. 250	10–15 minutes	L2
—— Cooperative Learning Activity, TWE, p. 251	10–15 minutes	L1
—— Graphic Organizer Transparencies and Strategies 8, TCR 🖨 📁	20–25 minutes	All levels
—— Cooperative Learning Activity 8, TCR 📁	20–25 minutes	All levels

Independent Practice

—— Guided Reading Activity 8-1, TCR 📁	15–20 minutes	All levels
—— Audio Program 🎧	15–20 minutes	All levels
—— Linking Past and Present Activity 8, TCR 📁	15–20 minutes	L2

ASSESS MENU

Evaluate

—— Reading Essentials and Study Guide 8-1, TCR 📁	25–35 minutes	L1, ELL
—— Section Quiz 8-1, TCR 📁	10–15 minutes	All levels
—— MindJogger Videoquiz, Chapter 8 📼	20–25 minutes	All levels

Reteach

—— Reteaching Activity, TWE, p. 252	10–15 minutes	L1, ELL

Enrich

—— Enrich, TWE, p. 249	5–10 minutes	L1
—— Enrichment Activity 8, TCR 📁	10–15 minutes	L2

CLOSE MENU

—— Close, TWE, p. 252	10–15 minutes	L1

See Optional Resources menu on page viii.

The Mongols and China
Section 2 (*pp. 253–257*)

LOCAL OBJECTIVES	TWE—Teacher Wraparound Edition TCR—Teacher Classroom Resources 📁 Blackline Master 🖐 Transparency 💿 CD-ROM 🎧 Audio Program 📼 Videocassette 🖱 Internet Resources		

OBJECTIVES

1. The Mongols acquired the world's largest land empire.

2. With the invention of printing, a golden age of literature and art emerged in China.

FOCUS MENU	SUGGESTED TIME RANGES	SUGGESTED LEVEL
—— Bellringer Skillbuilder Activity, TWE, p. 253; used with Daily Focus Skills Transparency or Blackline Master 8-2, TCR 🖐 📁	5–10 minutes	L1
—— Guide to Reading, TWE, p. 253	15–20 minutes	All levels
—— Vocabulary PuzzleMaker	15–20 minutes	All levels

TEACH MENU

Guided Practice

—— History Online Student Web Activity 8 🖱		
—— Cooperative Learning Activity, TWE, p. 254	25–30 minutes	L1
—— Connecting Across Time, TWE, p. 255	5–10 minutes	L1
—— Connecting Across Time, TWE, p. 256	25–30 minutes	L2
—— Critical Thinking Activity, TWE, p. 256	10–15 minutes	L2
—— Graphic Organizer Transparencies and Strategies 8, TCR 🖐 📁	20–25 minutes	All levels

Independent Practice

—— Guided Reading Activity 8-2, TCR 📁	15–20 minutes	L1, ELL
—— Audio Program 🎧	20–25 minutes	All levels, ELL
—— Historical Significance Activity 8, TCR 📁	10–15 minutes	L1
—— Critical Thinking Activity 8, TCR 📁	10–15 minutes	L1

ASSESS MENU

Evaluate

—— Reading Essentials and Study Guide 8-2, TCR 📁	25–35 minutes	L1, ELL
—— Section Quiz 8-2, TCR 📁	10–15 minutes	All levels
—— Interactive Tutor Self-Assessment CD-ROM, TCR 💿	20–30 minutes	All levels

Reteach

—— Reteaching Activity, TWE, p. 257	10–15 minutes	L1, ELL

CLOSE MENU

—— Close, TWE, p. 257	5–10 minutes	L1

See Optional Resources menu on page viii.

Early Japan and Korea

Section 3 *(pp. 263–267)*

LOCAL OBJECTIVES	TWE—Teacher Wraparound Edition TCR—Teacher Classroom Resources 📁 Blackline Master 📇 Transparency 💿 CD-ROM 🔊 Audio Program 📼 Videocassette 🖱 Internet Resources		

OBJECTIVES

1. Japan developed differently from many other countries because of its geography.
2. Japan's history has been marked by power struggles between rulers and independent families.

FOCUS MENU		SUGGESTED TIME RANGES	SUGGESTED LEVEL
—— Bellringer Skillbuilder Activity, TWE, p. 263; used with Daily Focus Skills Transparency or Blackline Master 8-3, TCR 📇 📁		5–10 minutes	L1
—— Guide to Reading, TWE, p. 263		5–10 minutes	All levels
—— Vocabulary PuzzleMaker 💿		15–20 minutes	All levels

TEACH MENU

Guided Practice

—— Writing Activity, TWE, p. 265		25–30 minutes	L1
—— Critical Thinking Activity, TWE, p. 265		25–30 minutes	L3
—— Cooperative Learning Activity, TWE, p. 266		25–30 minutes	L2
—— Critical Thinking, TWE, p. 267		10–15 minutes	L2
—— Graphic Organizer Transparencies and Strategies 8, TCR 📇 📁		20–25 minutes	All levels

Independent Practice

—— Guided Reading Activity 8-3, TCR 📁		15–20 minutes	L1, ELL
—— Audio Program 🔊		20–25 minutes	All levels, ELL

ASSESS MENU

Evaluate

—— Reading Essentials and Study Guide 8-3, TCR 📁		25–35 minutes	L1, ELL
—— Section Quiz 8-3, TCR 📁		10–15 minutes	All levels
—— Interactive Tutor Self-Assessment CD-ROM, TCR 💿		20–30 minutes	All levels

Reteach

—— Reteaching Activity, TWE, p. 267		10–15 minutes	L1, ELL

Enrich

—— Enrich, TWE, p. 265		5–10 minutes	L2

CLOSE MENU

—— Close, TWE, p. 267		5–10 minutes	L1

See Optional Resources menu on page viii.

India after the Guptas

Section 4 *(pp. 268–272)*

LOCAL OBJECTIVES	TWE—Teacher Wraparound Edition TCR—Teacher Classroom Resources ▭ Blackline Master 🖋 Transparency ◉ CD-ROM 🎧 Audio Program ▥ Videocassette ⬤ Internet Resources		
	OBJECTIVES **1.** Buddhism, Hinduism, and Islam influenced the development of India. **2.** Its location made India a center for trade, but conflicts among its states plagued its growth and prosperity.		
	FOCUS MENU	**SUGGESTED TIME RANGES**	**SUGGESTED LEVEL**
	—— Bellringer Skillbuilder Activity, TWE, p. 268; used with Daily Focus Skills Transparency or Blackline Master 8-4, TCR 🖋 ▭	5–10 minutes	L1
	—— Guide to Reading, TWE, p. 268	5–10 minutes	All levels
	—— Vocabulary PuzzleMaker	15–20 minutes	All levels
	TEACH MENU **Guided Practice**		
	—— Connecting Across Time, TWE, p. 269	10–15 minutes	L2
	—— Critical Thinking Activity, TWE, p. 269	20–25 minutes	L2
	—— Cooperative Learning Activity, TWE, p. 270	20–25 minutes	L2
	—— Graphic Organizer Transparencies and Strategies 8, TCR 🖋 ▭	20–25 minutes	All levels
	Independent Practice		
	—— Guided Reading Activity 8-4, TCR ▭	15–20 minutes	L1, ELL
	—— Audio Program 🎧	20–25 minutes	All levels, ELL
	ASSESS MENU **Evaluate**		
	—— Reading Essentials and Study Guide 8-4, TCR ▭	25–35 minutes	L1, ELL
	—— Section Quiz 8-4, TCR ▭	10–15 minutes	All levels
	—— Interactive Tutor Self-Assessment CD-ROM, TCR ◉	20–30 minutes	All levels
	Reteach		
	—— Reteaching Activity, TWE, p. 272	5–10 minutes	L1, ELL
	Enrich		
	—— Enrich, TWE, p. 271	5–10 minutes	L2
	CLOSE MENU		
	—— Close, TWE, p. 272	5–10 minutes	L1

See Optional Resources menu on page viii.

Grade _____ Class(es) _____ Date _____ M Tu W Th F

Teacher's Name _____ Date _____

Civilization in Southeast Asia   Section 5 *(pp. 273–278)*

LOCAL OBJECTIVES	TWE—Teacher Wraparound Edition TCR—Teacher Classroom Resources Blackline Master Transparency CD-ROM Audio Program Videocassette Internet Resources		
	OBJECTIVES **1.** Geography and cultural influences affected the development of Southeast Asia. **2.** Southeast Asian countries had primarily farming or trading economies that influenced their social structures.		
	FOCUS MENU	**SUGGESTED TIME RANGES**	**SUGGESTED LEVEL**
	—— Bellringer Skillbuilder Activity, TWE, p. 273; used with Daily Focus Skills Transparency or Blackline Master 8-5, TCR	5–10 minutes	L1
	—— Guide to Reading, TWE, p. 273	10–15 minutes	All levels
	—— Vocabulary PuzzleMaker	15–20 minutes	All levels
	TEACH MENU **Guided Practice**		
	—— Critical Thinking, TWE, p. 274	5–10 minutes	L1
	—— Critical Thinking Activity, TWE, p. 275	20–25 minutes	L2
	—— Writing Activity, TWE, p. 276	15–20 minutes	L2
	—— Cooperative Learning Activity, TWE, p. 276	25–30 minutes	L2
	—— Interdisciplinary Connections Activity, TWE, p. 277	20–25 minutes	L2
	—— Graphic Organizer Transparencies and Strategies 8, TCR	20–25 minutes	All levels
	—— History Simulation 8, TCR	30–35 minutes	All levels
	Independent Practice		
	—— Guided Reading Activity 8-5, TCR	15–20 minutes	L1, ELL
	—— Skills Reinforcement Activity 8, TCR	15–20 minutes	All levels
	—— Primary Source Reading 8, TCR	20–25 minutes	L2
	—— Time Line Activity 8, TCR	10–15 minutes	L2
	ASSESS MENU **Evaluate**		
	—— Reading Essentials and Study Guide 8-5, TCR	25–35 minutes	L1, ELL
	—— Section Quiz 8-5, TCR	25–30 minutes	All levels
	—— Chapter 8 Tests, TCR		
	—— Interactive Tutor Self-Assessment CD-ROM, TCR	20–30 minutes	All levels
	—— History Online Self-Check Quiz 8	15–20 minutes	All levels
	—— Performance Assessment Activity 8, TCR	20–25 minutes	All levels
	Reteach		
	—— Reteaching Activity, TWE, p. 278	5–10 minutes	L1, ELL
	—— Reteaching Activity 8, TCR	15–20 minutes	L1
	Enrich		
	—— Enrich, TWE, p. 276	20–25 minutes	L1
	CLOSE MENU —— Close, TWE, p. 278	5–10 minutes	L1

See Optional Resources menu on page viii.

Grade _____ Class(es) _____ Date _____ M Tu W Th F

Teacher's Name _____ Date _____

Transforming the Roman World   Section 1 (pp. 285–290)

LOCAL OBJECTIVES	TWE—Teacher Wraparound Edition TCR—Teacher Classroom Resources 🗁 Blackline Master ✒ Transparency 💿 CD-ROM 🎧 Audio Program 📼 Videocassette 🖰 Internet Resources

OBJECTIVES
1. The new European civilization was formed by the Germanic peoples, the legacy of the Romans, and the Church.
2. Charlemagne expanded the Frankish kingdom and created the Carolingian Empire.

FOCUS MENU	SUGGESTED TIME RANGES	SUGGESTED LEVEL
—— Bellringer Skillbuilder Activity, TWE, p. 285; used with Daily Focus Skills Transparency or Blackline Master 9-1, TCR ✒ 🗁	5–10 minutes	L1
—— Guide to Reading, TWE, p. 285	15–20 minutes	All levels
—— Vocabulary Activity 9, TCR 🗁	10–15 minutes	All levels
—— Vocabulary PuzzleMaker 💿	15–20 minutes	All levels
—— History Online Chapter 9 Overview 🖰	10–15 minutes	L1

TEACH MENU
Guided Practice

—— Writing Activity, TWE, p. 286	20–25 minutes	L2
—— Critical Thinking Activity, TWE, p. 193	10–15 minutes	L2
—— Connecting Across Time, TWE, p. 287	10–15 minutes	L2
—— Critical Thinking, TWE, p. 287	5–10 minutes	L2
—— Interdisciplinary Connections Activity, TWE, p. 288	15–20 minutes	L2
—— Meeting Individual Needs, TWE, p. 289	20–25 minutes	L1, ELL
—— Graphic Organizer Transparencies and Strategies 9, TCR ✒ 🗁	20–25 minutes	All levels

Independent Practice

—— Guided Reading Activity 9-1, TCR 🗁	15–20 minutes	All levels
—— Audio Program 🎧	15–20 minutes	All levels

ASSESS MENU
Evaluate

—— Reading Essentials and Study Guide 9-1, TCR 🗁	25–35 minutes	L1, ELL
—— Section Quiz 9-1, TCR 🗁	10–15 minutes	All levels
—— Interactive Tutor Self-Assessment CD-ROM, TCR 💿	20–30 minutes	All levels
—— MindJogger Videoquiz, Chapter 9 📼	20–25 minutes	All levels

Reteach

—— Reteaching Activity, TWE, p. 290	10–15 minutes	L1, ELL

Enrich

—— Enrich, TWE, p. 286	20–25 minutes	L2
—— Enrich, TWE, p. 288	5–10 minutes	L2

CLOSE MENU

—— Close, TWE, p. 290	10–15 minutes	L1

See Optional Resources menu on page viii.

Grade _____   Class(es) _____   Date _____   M Tu W Th F

Teacher's Name _____   Date _____

Feudalism

Section 2 (pp. 291–296)

LOCAL OBJECTIVES	TWE—Teacher Wraparound Edition 📁 Blackline Master 🖋 Transparency 🎧 Audio Program 📼 Videocassette	TCR—Teacher Classroom Resources 💿 CD-ROM 🖱 Internet Resources

OBJECTIVES

1. Vikings, Magyars, and Muslims invaded Europe during the ninth and tenth centuries.
2. The collapse of central authority in the European world led to a new political system known as feudalism.

FOCUS MENU	**SUGGESTED TIME RANGES**	**SUGGESTED LEVEL**
—— Bellringer Skillbuilder Activity, TWE, p. 291; used with Daily Focus Skills Transparency or Blackline Master 9-2, TCR 🖋 📁	5–10 minutes	L1
—— Guide to Reading, TWE, p. 291	15–20 minutes	All levels
—— Vocabulary PuzzleMaker 💿	15–20 minutes	All levels

TEACH MENU

Guided Practice

—— Connecting Across Time, TWE, p. 292	10–15 minutes	L2
—— Cooperative Learning Activity, TWE, p. 292	25–30 minutes	L1, ELL
—— Writing Activity, TWE, p. 293	15–20 minutes	L2
—— Critical Thinking Activity, TWE, p. 293	5–10 minutes	L2
—— History Online Student Web Activity 9 🖱		
—— Writing Activity, TWE, p. 294	20–25 minutes	L2
—— Cooperative Learning Activity, TWE, p. 294	30–35 minutes	L1, ELL
—— Graphic Organizer Transparencies and Strategies 9, TCR 🖋 📁	20–25 minutes	All levels

Independent Practice

—— Guided Reading Activity 9-2, TCR 📁	15–20 minutes	L1, ELL
—— Audio Program 🎧	20–25 minutes	All levels, ELL

ASSESS MENU

Evaluate

—— Reading Essentials and Study Guide 9-2, TCR 📁	25–35 minutes	L1, ELL
—— Section Quiz 9-2, TCR 📁	10–15 minutes	All levels
—— Interactive Tutor Self-Assessment CD-ROM, TCR 💿	20–30 minutes	All levels

Reteach

—— Reteaching Activity, TWE, p. 296	5–10 minutes	L1, ELL

Enrich

—— Enrich, TWE, p. 293	10–15 minutes	L2

CLOSE MENU

—— Close, TWE, p. 296	5–10 minutes	L1

See Optional Resources menu on page viii.

The Growth of European Kingdoms   Section 3 *(pp. 297–301)*

LOCAL OBJECTIVES	TWE—Teacher Wraparound Edition TCR—Teacher Classroom Resources 📁 Blackline Master 🖨 Transparency 💿 CD-ROM 🎧 Audio Program 📼 Videocassette ⌁ Internet Resources

	OBJECTIVES
	1. During the High Middle Ages, European monarchs began to extend their power and build strong states.
	2. The Slavic peoples formed three distinct groups, and they settled in different parts of eastern Europe.

	FOCUS MENU	**SUGGESTED TIME RANGES**	**SUGGESTED LEVEL**
	—— Bellringer Skillbuilder Activity, TWE, p. 297; used with Daily Focus Skills Transparency or Blackline Master 9-3, TCR 🖨 📁	5–10 minutes	L1
	—— Guide to Reading, TWE, p. 297	5–10 minutes	All levels
	—— Vocabulary PuzzleMaker 💿	15–20 minutes	All levels
	TEACH MENU		
	Guided Practice		
	—— Interdisciplinary Connections Activity, TWE, p. 298	20–25 minutes	L2
	—— Cooperative Learning Activity, TWE, p. 300	30–35 minutes	L2
	—— Graphic Organizer Transparencies and Strategies 9, TCR 🖨 📁	20–25 minutes	All levels
	Independent Practice		
	—— Guided Reading Activity 9-3, TCR 📁	15–20 minutes	L1, ELL
	—— Audio Program 🎧	20–25 minutes	All levels, ELL
	—— Linking Past and Present Activity 9, TCR 📁	15–20 minutes	L2
	—— Critical Thinking Skills Activity 9, TCR 📁	10–15 minutes	L2
	ASSESS MENU		
	Evaluate		
	—— Reading Essentials and Study Guide 9-3, TCR 📁	25–35 minutes	L1, ELL
	—— Section Quiz 9-3, TCR 📁	10–15 minutes	All levels
	—— Interactive Tutor Self-Assessment CD-ROM, TCR 💿	20–30 minutes	All levels
	—— Performance Assessment Activity 9, TCR 📁	20–25 minutes	All levels
	Reteach		
	—— Reteaching Activity, TWE, p. 301	5–10 minutes	L1, ELL
	Enrich		
	—— Enrich, TWE, p. 299	10–15 minutes	L2
	CLOSE MENU		
	—— Close, TWE, p. 301	5–10 minutes	L1

See Optional Resources menu on page viii.

The Byzantine Empire and the Crusades

Section 4 *(pp. 303–308)*

LOCAL OBJECTIVES	TWE—Teacher Wraparound Edition TCR—Teacher Classroom Resources 📁 Blackline Master 🔲 Transparency 💿 CD-ROM 🎧 Audio Program 📼 Videocassette ●⌐ Internet Resources		
	OBJECTIVES **1.** The Byzantine Empire created its own unique civilization in the eastern Mediterranean. **2.** The Crusades impacted medieval society in both the East and the West.		
	FOCUS MENU	**SUGGESTED TIME RANGES**	**SUGGESTED LEVEL**
	—— Bellringer Skillbuilder Activity, TWE, p. 303; used with Daily Focus Skills Transparency or Blackline Master 9-4, TCR 🔲 📁	5–10 minutes	L1
	—— Guide to Reading, TWE, p. 303	10–15 minutes	All levels
	—— Vocabulary PuzzleMaker 💿	15–20 minutes	All levels
	TEACH MENU **Guided Practice**		
	—— Cooperative Learning Activity, TWE, p. 304	25–30 minutes	L2
	—— Critical Thinking, TWE, p. 306	10–15 minutes	L3
	—— Graphic Organizer Transparencies and Strategies 9, TCR 🔲 📁	20–25 minutes	All levels
	—— Cooperative Learning Activity 9, TCR 📁	20–25 minutes	All levels
	—— History Simulation 9, TCR 📁	25–30 minutes	All levels
	Independent Practice		
	—— Guided Reading Activity 9-4, TCR 📁	15–20 minutes	L1, ELL
	—— Skills Reinforcement Activity 9, TCR 📁	15–20 minutes	All levels
	—— Primary Source Reading 9, TCR 📁	20–25 minutes	L3
	—— Historical Significance Activity 9, TCR 📁	10–15 minutes	L1
	—— Time Line Activity 9, TCR 📁	10–15 minutes	L2
	ASSESS MENU **Evaluate**		
	—— Reading Essentials and Study Guide 9-4, TCR 📁	25–35 minutes	L1, ELL
	—— Section Quiz 9-4, TCR 📁	25–30 minutes	All levels
	—— Chapter 9 Tests, TCR 📁		
	—— History Online Self-Check Quiz 9 ●⌐	15–20 minutes	All levels
	Reteach		
	—— Reteaching Activity, TWE, p. 308	15–20 minutes	L1, ELL
	—— Reteaching Activity 9, TCR 📁	15–20 minutes	L1
	Enrich		
	—— Enrich, TWE, p. 306	10–15 minutes	L1, ELL
	—— Enrichment Activity 9, TCR 📁	10–15 minutes	L2
	CLOSE MENU —— Close, TWE, p. 308	10–15 minutes	L1

See Optional Resources menu on page viii.

Peasants, Trade, and Cities   Section 1 *(pp. 315–322)*

LOCAL OBJECTIVES	TWE—Teacher Wraparound Edition TCR—Teacher Classroom Resources		
	📁 Blackline Master ✊ Transparency 💿 CD-ROM		
	🎧 Audio Program 📺 Videocassette ➥ Internet Resources		

OBJECTIVES

1. New farming practices, the growth of trade, and the rise of cities created a flourishing European society.
2. The revival of trade and the development of a money economy offered new opportunities for people.

FOCUS MENU	**SUGGESTED TIME RANGES**	**SUGGESTED LEVEL**
—— Bellringer Skillbuilder Activity, TWE, p. 315; used with Daily Focus Skills Transparency or Blackline Master 10-1, TCR ✊ 📁	5–10 minutes	L1
—— Guide to Reading, TWE, p. 315	15–20 minutes	All levels
—— Vocabulary Activity 10, TCR 📁	10–15 minutes	All levels
—— Vocabulary PuzzleMaker 💿	15–20 minutes	All levels
—— History Online Chapter 10 Overview ➥	10–15 minutes	L1

TEACH MENU		
Guided Practice		
—— Critical Thinking, TWE, p. 316	5–10 minutes	L1
—— Meeting Individual Needs, TWE, p. 316	10–15 minutes	L1
—— Charting Activity, TWE, p. 317	15–20 minutes	L2
—— Connecting Across Time, TWE, p. 318	10–15 minutes	L2
—— Cooperative Learning Activity, TWE, p. 318	30–35 minutes	L2, ELL
—— Critical Thinking Activity, TWE, p. 319	10–15 minutes	L2
—— Interdisciplinary Connections Activity, TWE, p. 320	15–20 minutes	L2
—— Writing Activity, TWE, p. 321	15–20 minutes	L2
—— Graphic Organizer Transparencies and Strategies 10, TCR ✊ 📁	20–25 minutes	All levels
—— History Simulation 10, TCR 📁	20–25 minutes	All levels
Independent Practice		
—— Guided Reading Activity 10-1, TCR 📁	15–20 minutes	All levels
—— Historical Significance Activity 10, TCR 📁	10–15 minutes	L2

ASSESS MENU		
Evaluate		
—— Reading Essentials and Study Guide 10-1, TCR 📁	25–35 minutes	L1, ELL
—— Section Quiz 10-1, TCR 📁	10–15 minutes	All levels
Reteach		
—— Reteaching Activity, TWE, p. 322	10–15 minutes	L1, ELL
Enrich		
—— Enrich, TWE, p. 318	10–15 minutes	L2
—— Enrichment Activity 10, TCR 📁	15–20 minutes	L2

CLOSE MENU		
—— Close, TWE, p. 322	5–10 minutes	L1

See Optional Resources menu on page viii.

Christianity and Medieval Civilization Section 2 *(pp. 323–328)*

LOCAL OBJECTIVES	TWE—Teacher Wraparound Edition 📁 Blackline Master 🖋 Transparency 🎧 Audio Program 📼 Videocassette	TCR—Teacher Classroom Resources 💿 CD-ROM 🖱 Internet Resources		
	OBJECTIVES **1.** The Catholic Church played a dominant role in the lives of people during the High Middle Ages. **2.** Strong leadership by the popes made the Catholic Church a forceful presence in medieval society.			
	FOCUS MENU		**SUGGESTED TIME RANGES**	**SUGGESTED LEVEL**
	—— Bellringer Skillbuilder Activity, TWE, p. 323; used with Daily Focus Skills Transparency or Blackline Master 10-2, TCR 🖋 📁		5–10 minutes	L1
	—— Guide to Reading, TWE, p. 323		15–20 minutes	All levels
	—— Vocabulary PuzzleMaker 💿		15–20 minutes	All levels
	TEACH MENU **Guided Practice**			
	—— Connecting Across Time, TWE, p. 324		10–15 minutes	L2
	—— Cooperative Learning Activity, TWE, p. 324		25–30 minutes	L2
	—— Critical Thinking Activity, TWE, p. 325		15–20 minutes	L3
	—— Writing Activity, TWE, p. 326		20–25 minutes	L2
	—— Interdisciplinary Connections Activity, TWE, p. 326		20–25 minutes	L2
	—— Graphic Organizer Transparencies and Strategies 10, TCR 🖋 📁		20–25 minutes	All levels
	Independent Practice			
	—— Guided Reading Activity 10-2, TCR 📁		15–20 minutes	L1, ELL
	—— Audio Program 🎧		20–25 minutes	All levels, ELL
	—— Critical Thinking Skills Activity 10, TCR 📁		15–20 minutes	L2
	ASSESS MENU **Evaluate**			
	—— Reading Essentials and Study Guide 10-2, TCR 📁		25–35 minutes	L1, ELL
	—— Section Quiz 10-2, TCR 📁		10–15 minutes	All levels
	—— Interactive Tutor Self-Assessment CD-ROM, TCR 💿		20–30 minutes	All levels
	Reteach			
	—— Reteaching Activity, TWE, p. 328		10–15 minutes	L1, ELL
	Enrich			
	—— Enrich, TWE, p. 325		10–15 minutes	L2
	CLOSE MENU			
	—— Close, TWE, p. 328		5–10 minutes	L1

See Optional Resources menu on page viii.

The Culture of the High Middle Ages Section 3 *(pp. 329–333)*

LOCAL OBJECTIVES	TWE—Teacher Wraparound Edition 📁 Blackline Master 🔥 Transparency 🔊 Audio Program 📼 Videocassette	TCR—Teacher Classroom Resources 💿 CD-ROM ⌐ Internet Resources

	OBJECTIVES **1.** An intellectual revival led to the formation of universities. **2.** In the High Middle Ages, new technical innovations made it possible to build Gothic cathedrals, which are one of the great artistic triumphs of this age.		

	FOCUS MENU	**SUGGESTED TIME RANGES**	**SUGGESTED LEVEL**
	—— Bellringer Skillbuilder Activity, TWE, p. 329; used with Daily Focus Skills Transparency or Blackline Master 10-3, TCR 🔥 📁	5–10 minutes	L1
	—— Guide to Reading, TWE, p. 329	5–10 minutes	All levels
	—— Vocabulary PuzzleMaker 💿	15–20 minutes	All levels
	TEACH MENU **Guided Practice**		
	—— Connecting Across Time, TWE, p. 330	10–15 minutes	L1
	—— Interdisciplinary Connections Activity, TWE, p. 331	25–30 minutes	L3
	—— Critical Thinking, TWE, p. 332	10–15 minutes	L2
	—— History Online Student Web Activity 10 ⌐		
	—— Graphic Organizer Transparencies and Strategies 10, TCR 🔥 📁	20–25 minutes	All levels
	—— Cooperative Learning Activity 10, TCR 📁	20–25 minutes	All levels
	Independent Practice		
	—— Guided Reading Activity 10-3, TCR 📁	15–20 minutes	L1, ELL
	—— Audio Program 🔊	20–25 minutes	All levels, ELL
	—— Skills Reinforcement Activity 10, TCR 📁	15–20 minutes	All levels
	ASSESS MENU **Evaluate**		
	—— Reading Essentials and Study Guide 10-3, TCR 📁	25–35 minutes	L1, ELL
	—— Section Quiz 10-3, TCR 📁	10–15 minutes	All levels
	—— Interactive Tutor Self-Assessment CD-ROM, TCR 💿	20–30 minutes	All levels
	—— Performance Assessment Activity 10, TCR 📁	20–25 minutes	All levels
	Reteach		
	—— Reteaching Activity, TWE, p. 333	10–15 minutes	L1, ELL
	CLOSE MENU		
	—— Close, TWE, p. 333	5–10 minutes	L1

See Optional Resources menu on page viii.

The Late Middle Ages
Section 4 (pp. 335–340)

LOCAL OBJECTIVES	TWE—Teacher Wraparound Edition TCR—Teacher Classroom Resources 📁 Blackline Master 🔥 Transparency 💿 CD-ROM 🎧 Audio Program 📼 Videocassette 🖱 Internet Resources		
	OBJECTIVES **1.** Europe in the fourteenth century was challenged by an overwhelming number of disastrous forces. **2.** European rulers reestablished the centralized power of monarchical governments.		
	FOCUS MENU	**SUGGESTED TIME RANGES**	**SUGGESTED LEVEL**
	—— Bellringer Skillbuilder Activity, TWE, p. 335; used with Daily Focus Skills Transparency or Blackline Master 10-4, TCR 🔥 📁	5–10 minutes	L1
	—— Guide to Reading, TWE, p. 335	10–15 minutes	All levels
	—— Vocabulary PuzzleMaker 💿	15–20 minutes	All levels
	TEACH MENU **Guided Practice**		
	—— Cooperative Learning Activity, TWE, p. 336	25–30 minutes	L2
	—— Connecting Across Time, TWE, p. 337	15–20 minutes	L2
	—— Writing Activity, TWE, p. 338	15–20 minutes	L1
	—— Critical Thinking Activity, TWE, p. 338	15–20 minutes	L2
	—— Interdisciplinary Connections Activity, TWE, p. 339	25–30 minutes	L3
	—— Graphic Organizer Transparencies and Strategies 10, TCR 🔥 📁	20–25 minutes	All levels
	Independent Practice		
	—— Guided Reading Activity 10-4, TCR 📁	15–20 minutes	L1, ELL
	—— Audio Program 🎧	20–25 minutes	All levels, ELL
	—— Linking Past and Present Activity 10, TCR 📁	15–20 minutes	L2
	—— Primary Source Reading 10, TCR 📁	20–25 minutes	L2
	—— Time Line Activity 10, TCR 📁	10–15 minutes	L2
	ASSESS MENU **Evaluate**		
	—— Reading Essentials and Study Guide 10-4, TCR 📁	25–35 minutes	L1, ELL
	—— Section Quiz 10-4, TCR 📁	25–30 minutes	All levels
	—— Chapter 10 Tests, TCR 📁		
	—— Interactive Tutor Self-Assessment CD-ROM, TCR 💿	20–30 minutes	All levels
	—— MindJogger Videoquiz, Chapter 10 📼	20–25 minutes	All levels
	—— History Online Self-Check Quiz 10 🖱	15–20 minutes	All levels
	Reteach		
	—— Reteaching Activity, TWE, p. 340	5–10 minutes	L1, ELL
	—— Reteaching Activity 10, TCR 📁	15–20 minutes	L1
	CLOSE MENU —— Close, TWE, p. 340	5–10 minutes	L1

See Optional Resources menu on page viii.

The Peoples of North America   Section 1 *(pp. 347–350)*

LOCAL OBJECTIVES	TWE—Teacher Wraparound Edition TCR—Teacher Classroom Resources 📁 Blackline Master 🖋 Transparency 💿 CD-ROM 🔊 Audio Program 📼 Videocassette 🖱 Internet Resources		
	OBJECTIVES **1.** The first inhabitants of the Americas were hunters and gatherers, while later inhabitants also practiced farming. **2.** Because of the great variety of climate and geographic features, many different cultures emerged in the Americas.		
	FOCUS MENU	**SUGGESTED TIME RANGES**	**SUGGESTED LEVEL**
	——— Bellringer Skillbuilder Activity, TWE, p. 347; used with Daily Focus Skills Transparency or Blackline Master 11-1, TCR 🖋 📁	5–10 minutes	L1
	——— Guide to Reading, TWE, p. 347	15–20 minutes	All levels
	——— Vocabulary Activity 11, TCR 📁	10–15 minutes	All levels
	——— Vocabulary PuzzleMaker 💿	15–20 minutes	All levels
	——— History Online Chapter 11 Overview 🖱	10–15 minutes	L1
	TEACH MENU **Guided Practice**		
	——— Meeting Individual Needs, TWE, p. 349	20–25 minutes	L1, ELL
	——— Writing Activity, TWE, p. 350	20–25 minutes	L2
	——— Graphic Organizer Transparencies and Strategies 11, TCR 🖋 📁	20–25 minutes	All levels
	——— Cooperative Learning Activity 11, TCR 📁	20–25 minutes	All levels
	Independent Practice		
	——— Guided Reading Activity 11-1, TCR 📁	15–20 minutes	All levels
	——— Skills Reinforcement Activity 11, TCR 📁	15–20 minutes	All levels
	——— Audio Program 🔊	15–20 minutes	All levels
	——— Primary Source Reading 11, TCR 📁	20–25 minutes	L2
	——— Historical Significance Activity 11, TCR 📁	15–20 minutes	L1
	ASSESS MENU **Evaluate**		
	——— Reading Essentials and Study Guide 11-1, TCR 📁	25–35 minutes	L1, ELL
	——— Section Quiz 11-1, TCR 📁	10–15 minutes	All levels
	——— Interactive Tutor Self-Assessment CD-ROM, TCR 💿	20–30 minutes	All levels
	——— MindJogger Videoquiz, Chapter 11 📼	20–25 minutes	All levels
	Reteach		
	——— Reteaching Activity, TWE, p. 350	10–15 minutes	L1, ELL
	Enrich		
	——— Enrich, TWE, p. 349	15–20 minutes	L3
	CLOSE MENU		
	——— Close, TWE, p. 350	10–15 minutes	L1

See Optional Resources menu on page viii.

Grade _____ Class(es) _____ Date _____ M Tu W Th F

Teacher's Name _____ Date _____

Early Civilizations in Mesoamerica   Section 2 (pp. 352–358)

LOCAL OBJECTIVES	TWE—Teacher Wraparound Edition TCR—Teacher Classroom Resources 📁 Blackline Master 🖌 Transparency 💿 CD-ROM 🎧 Audio Program 📼 Videocassette 🖱 Internet Resources		
	OBJECTIVES **1.** Early Mesoamerican civilizations flourished with fully-developed political, religious, and social structures. **2.** The Aztec state succumbed to diseases brought by the Spanish.		
	FOCUS MENU	**SUGGESTED TIME RANGES**	**SUGGESTED LEVEL**
	—— Bellringer Skillbuilder Activity, TWE, p. 352; used with Daily Focus Skills Transparency or Blackline Master 11-2, TCR 🖌 📁	5–10 minutes	L1
	—— Guide to Reading, TWE, p. 352	15–20 minutes	All levels
	—— Vocabulary PuzzleMaker 💿	15–20 minutes	All levels
	TEACH MENU **Guided Practice**		
	—— Writing Activity, TWE, p. 353	15–20 minutes	L1
	—— Cooperative Learning Activity, TWE, p. 354	25–30 minutes	L2
	—— Connecting Across Time, TWE, p. 355	5–10 minutes	L1
	—— Interdisciplinary Connections Activity, TWE, p. 355	25–30 minutes	L3
	—— Connecting Across Time, TWE, p. 356	20–25 minutes	L2
	—— Critical Thinking Activity, TWE, p. 356	15–20 minutes	L2
	—— Writing Activity, TWE, p. 358	20–25 minutes	L1
	—— History Online Student Web Activity 11 🖱		
	—— Graphic Organizer Transparencies and Strategies 11, TCR 🖌 📁	20–25 minutes	All levels
	Independent Practice		
	—— Guided Reading Activity 11-2, TCR 📁	15–20 minutes	L1, ELL
	—— Audio Program 🎧	20–25 minutes	All levels, ELL
	—— Linking Past and Present Activity 11, TCR 📁	15–20 minutes	L2
	—— Time Line Activity 11, TCR 📁	10–15 minutes	L2
	—— Critical Thinking Activity 11, TCR 📁	15–20 minutes	L2
	ASSESS MENU **Evaluate**		
	—— Reading Essentials and Study Guide 11-2, TCR 📁	25–35 minutes	L1, ELL
	—— Section Quiz 11-2, TCR 📁	10–15 minutes	All levels
	—— Interactive Tutor Self-Assessment CD-ROM, TCR 💿	20–30 minutes	All levels
	Reteach		
	—— Reteaching Activity, TWE, p. 358	10–15 minutes	L1, ELL
	Enrich		
	—— Enrich, TWE, p. 354	10–15 minutes	L1
	—— Enrichment Activity 11, TCR 📁	10–15 minutes	L2
	CLOSE MENU		
	—— Close, TWE, p. 358	10–15 minutes	L1

See Optional Resources menu on page viii.

Grade _____ Class(es) _____ Date _____ M Tu W Th F

Teacher's Name _____ Date _____

Early Civilizations in South America Section 3 (pp. 359–362)

LOCAL OBJECTIVES	TWE—Teacher Wraparound Edition TCR—Teacher Classroom Resources 📁 Blackline Master 🖋 Transparency 💿 CD-ROM 🎧 Audio Program 📼 Videocassette 🖱 Internet Resources

	OBJECTIVES
	1. The Inca developed a well-organized, militaristic empire.
	2. Incan communities undertook sophisticated building projects and established a high level of cultural development.

	FOCUS MENU	**SUGGESTED TIME RANGES**	**SUGGESTED LEVEL**
	—— Bellringer Skillbuilder Activity, TWE, p. 359; used with Daily Focus Skills Transparency or Blackline Master 11-3, TCR 🖋 📁	5–10 minutes	L1
	—— Guide to Reading, TWE, p. 359	10–15 minutes	All levels
	—— Vocabulary PuzzleMaker 💿	15–20 minutes	All levels

	TEACH MENU		
	Guided Practice		
	—— Interdisciplinary Connections Activity, TWE, p. 361	25–30 minutes	L2
	—— Writing Activity, TWE, p. 361	15–20 minutes	L1
	—— Writing Activity, TWE, p. 362	25–30 minutes	L2
	—— Graphic Organizer Transparencies and Strategies 11, TCR 🖋 📁	20–25 minutes	All levels
	—— History Simulation 11, TCR 📁	30–35 minutes	All levels
	Independent Practice		
	—— Guided Reading Activity 11-3, TCR 📁	15–20 minutes	L1, ELL
	—— Audio Program 🎧	20–25 minutes	All levels, ELL

	ASSESS MENU		
	Evaluate		
	—— Reading Essentials and Study Guide 11-3, TCR 📁	25–35 minutes	L1, ELL
	—— Section Quiz 11-3, TCR 📁	25–30 minutes	All levels
	—— Chapter 11 Tests, TCR 📁		
	—— Interactive Tutor Self-Assessment CD-ROM, TCR 💿	20–30 minutes	All levels
	—— MindJogger Videoquiz, Chapter 11 📼	20–25 minutes	All levels
	—— History Online Self-Check Quiz 11 🖱	15–20 minutes	All levels
	—— Performance Assessment Activity 11, TCR 📁	15–20 minutes	All levels
	Reteach		
	—— Reteaching Activity, TWE, p. 362	10–15 minutes	L1, ELL
	—— Reteaching Activity 11, TCR 📁	15–20 minutes	L1
	Enrich		
	—— Enrich, TWE, p. 361	15–20 minutes	L1

	CLOSE MENU		
	—— Close, TWE, p. 362	5–10 minutes	L1

See Optional Resources menu on page viii.

The Renaissance

Section 1 *(pp. 375–381)*

LOCAL OBJECTIVES	TWE—Teacher Wraparound Edition TCR—Teacher Classroom Resources 📁 Blackline Master 📠 Transparency 💿 CD-ROM 🎧 Audio Program 📼 Videocassette 🖱 Internet Resources

	OBJECTIVES
	1. Between 1350 and 1550, Italian intellectuals believed they had entered a new age of human achievement.
	2. City-states were the centers of political, economic, and social life in Renaissance Italy.

	FOCUS MENU	**SUGGESTED TIME RANGES**	**SUGGESTED LEVEL**
	—— Bellringer Skillbuilder Activity, TWE, p. 375; used with Daily Focus Skills Transparency or Blackline Master 12-1, TCR 📠 📁	5–10 minutes	L1
	—— Guide to Reading, TWE, p. 375	15–20 minutes	All levels
	—— Vocabulary Activity 12, TCR 📁	10–15 minutes	All levels
	—— Vocabulary PuzzleMaker 💿	15–20 minutes	All levels
	—— History Online Chapter 12 Overview 🖱	10–15 minutes	L1

	TEACH MENU		
	Guided Practice		
	—— Cooperative Learning Activity, TWE, p. 376	20–25 minutes	L2
	—— Critical Thinking Activity, TWE, p. 377	15–20 minutes	L3
	—— Connecting Across Time, TWE, p. 378	5–10 minutes	L1
	—— Connecting Across Time, TWE, p. 379	10–15 minutes	L3
	—— Critical Thinking Activity, TWE, p. 379	25–30 minutes	L2
	—— Meeting Individual Needs, TWE, p. 380	15–20 minutes	L1
	—— Graphic Organizer Transparencies and Strategies 12, TCR 📠 📁	20–25 minutes	All levels
	—— Cooperative Learning Activity 12, TCR 📁	20–25 minutes	All levels
	Independent Practice		
	—— Guided Reading Activity 12-1, TCR 📁	15–20 minutes	All levels
	—— Audio Program 🎧	15–20 minutes	All levels
	—— Historical Significance Activity 12, TCR 📁	20–25 minutes	L3

	ASSESS MENU		
	Evaluate		
	—— Reading Essentials and Study Guide 12-1, TCR 📁	25–35 minutes	L1, ELL
	—— Section Quiz 12-1, TCR 📁	10–15 minutes	All levels
	—— Interactive Tutor Self-Assessment CD-ROM, TCR 💿	20–30 minutes	All levels
	—— MindJogger Videoquiz, Chapter 12 📼	20–25 minutes	All levels
	Reteach		
	—— Reteaching Activity, TWE, p. 381	10–15 minutes	L1
	Enrich		
	—— Enrich, TWE, p. 376	5–10 minutes	L2

	CLOSE MENU		
	—— Close, TWE, p. 381	5–10 minutes	L1

See Optional Resources menu on page viii.

The Intellectual and Artistic Renaissance

Section 2 (pp. 382–387)

LOCAL OBJECTIVES	TWE—Teacher Wraparound Edition TCR—Teacher Classroom Resources 🗄 Blackline Master 🖱 Transparency 💿 CD-ROM 🎧 Audio Program 📼 Videocassette 🖱 Internet Resources

	OBJECTIVES **1.** The most important intellectual movement associated with the Renaissance was humanism. **2.** The Renaissance produced many great artists and sculptors such as Michelangelo, Raphael, and Leonardo da Vinci.		

	FOCUS MENU	**SUGGESTED TIME RANGES**	**SUGGESTED LEVEL**
	____ Bellringer Skillbuilder Activity, TWE, p. 382; used with Daily Focus Skills Transparency or Blackline Master 12-2, TCR 🖱 🗄	5–10 minutes	L1
	____ Guide to Reading, TWE, p. 382	15–20 minutes	All levels
	____ Vocabulary PuzzleMaker 💿	15–20 minutes	All levels
	TEACH MENU **Guided Practice**		
	____ Interdisciplinary Connections Activity, TWE, p. 383	20–25 minutes	L2
	____ Critical Thinking, TWE, p. 384	15–20 minutes	L3
	____ Critical Thinking Activity, TWE, p. 384	15–20 minutes	L3
	____ Critical Thinking, TWE, p. 385	5–10 minutes	L1
	____ Cooperative Learning Activity, TWE, p. 386	30–35 minutes	L2
	____ Graphic Organizer Transparencies and Strategies 12, TCR 🖱 🗄	20–25 minutes	All levels
	____ History Simulation 12, TCR 🗄	25–30 minutes	All levels
	Independent Practice		
	____ Guided Reading Activity 12-2, TCR 🗄	15–20 minutes	L1, ELL
	____ Audio Program 🎧	20–25 minutes	All levels, ELL
	____ Linking Past and Present Activity 12, TCR 🗄	15–20 minutes	L2
	____ Primary Source Reading 12, TCR 🗄	20–25 minutes	L2
	____ Critical Thinking Skills Activity 12, TCR 🗄	10–15 minutes	L2
	ASSESS MENU **Evaluate**		
	____ Reading Essentials and Study Guide 12-2, TCR 🗄	25–35 minutes	L1, ELL
	____ Section Quiz 12-2, TCR 🗄	10–15 minutes	All levels
	____ Interactive Tutor Self-Assessment CD-ROM, TCR 💿	20–30 minutes	All levels
	____ Performance Assessment Activity 12, TCR 🗄	15–20 minutes	All levels
	Reteach ____ Reteaching Activity, TWE, p. 387	5–10 minutes	L2
	Enrich ____ Enrich, TWE, p. 385	25–30 minutes	L2
	CLOSE MENU ____ Close, TWE, p. 387	5–10 minutes	L1

See Optional Resources menu on page viii.

The Protestant Reformation   Section 3 *(pp. 389–393)*

LOCAL OBJECTIVES	TWE—Teacher Wraparound Edition TCR—Teacher Classroom Resources 📁 Blackline Master 🔧 Transparency 💿 CD-ROM 🔊 Audio Program 📼 Videocassette 🖱 Internet Resources		
	OBJECTIVES **1.** The major goal of humanism is northern Europe was to reform Christendom. **2.** Martin Luther's religious reforms led to the emergence of Protestantism.		
	FOCUS MENU	**SUGGESTED TIME RANGES**	**SUGGESTED LEVEL**
	—— Bellringer Skillbuilder Activity, TWE, p. 389; used with Daily Focus Skills Transparency or Blackline Master 12-3, TCR 🔧 📁	5–10 minutes	L1
	—— Guide to Reading, TWE, p. 389	5–10 minutes	All levels
	—— Vocabulary PuzzleMaker 💿	15–20 minutes	All levels
	TEACH MENU **Guided Practice**		
	—— Connecting Across Time, TWE, p. 390	10–15 minutes	L1
	—— Cooperative Learning Activity, TWE, p. 392	30–35 minutes	L2
	—— Graphic Organizer Transparencies and Strategies 12, TCR 🔧 📁	20–25 minutes	All levels
	Independent Practice		
	—— Guided Reading Activity 12-3, TCR 📁	15–20 minutes	L1, ELL
	—— Audio Program 🔊	20–25 minutes	All levels, ELL
	—— Skills Reinforcement Activity 12, TCR 📁	15–20 minutes	All levels
	ASSESS MENU **Evaluate**		
	—— Reading Essentials and Study Guide 12-3, TCR 📁	25–35 minutes	L1, ELL
	—— Section Quiz 12-3, TCR 📁	10–15 minutes	All levels
	—— Interactive Tutor Self-Assessment CD-ROM, TCR 💿	20–30 minutes	All levels
	Reteach		
	—— Reteaching Activity, TWE, p. 393	5–10 minutes	L1
	Enrich		
	—— Enrich, TWE, p. 392	15–20 minutes	L3
	—— Enrichment Activity 12, TCR 📁	15–20 minutes	L3
	CLOSE MENU		
	—— Close, TWE, p. 393	5–10 minutes	L2

See Optional Resources menu on page viii.

The Spread of Protestantism and the Catholic Response

Section 4 *(pp. 395–401)*

LOCAL OBJECTIVES	TWE—Teacher Wraparound Edition TCR—Teacher Classroom Resources
	📁 Blackline Master 🖋 Transparency 💿 CD-ROM
	🎧 Audio Program 📼 Videocassette 🖱 Internet Resources

OBJECTIVES

1. Different forms of Protestantism emerged in Europe as the Reformation spread.
2. The Catholic Church underwent a religious rebirth.

FOCUS MENU	SUGGESTED TIME RANGES	SUGGESTED LEVEL
—— Bellringer Skillbuilder Activity, TWE, p. 395; used with Daily Focus Skills Transparency or Blackline Master 12-4, TCR 🖋 📁	5–10 minutes	L1
—— Guide to Reading, TWE, p. 395	10–15 minutes	All levels
—— Vocabulary PuzzleMaker 💿	15–20 minutes	All levels

TEACH MENU
Guided Practice

—— Cooperative Learning Activity, TWE, p. 396	30–35 minutes	L2
—— Writing Activity, TWE, p. 398	15–20 minutes	L1
—— Meeting Individual Needs, TWE, p. 398	15–20 minutes	L1
—— Connecting Across Time, TWE, p. 399	15–20 minutes	L3
—— Critical Thinking Activity, TWE, p. 399	20–25 minutes	L1
—— Critical Thinking, TWE, p. 400	5–10 minutes	L2
—— Cooperative Learning Activity, TWE, p. 400	20–25 minutes	L1
—— History Online Student Web Activity 12 🖱		
—— Graphic Organizer Transparencies and Strategies 12, TCR 🖋 📁	20–25 minutes	All levels

Independent Practice

—— Guided Reading Activity 12-4, TCR 📁	15–20 minutes	L1, ELL
—— Audio Program 🎧	20–25 minutes	All levels, ELL
—— Time Line Activity 12, TCR 📁	10–15 minutes	L1

ASSESS MENU
Evaluate

—— Reading Essentials and Study Guide 12-4, TCR 📁	25–35 minutes	L1, ELL
—— Section Quiz 12-4, TCR 📁	25–30 minutes	All levels
—— Chapter 12 Tests, TCR 📁		
—— History Online Self-Check Quiz 12 🖱	15–20 minutes	All levels

Reteach

—— Reteaching Activity, TWE, p. 401	10–15 minutes	L1
—— Reteaching Activity 12, TCR 📁	15–20 minutes	L1

Enrich

—— Enrich, TWE, p. 398	10–15 minutes	L2

CLOSE MENU

—— Close, TWE, p. 401	5–10 minutes	L2

See Optional Resources menu on page viii.

Exploration and Expansion   Section 1 *(pp. 407–413)*

LOCAL OBJECTIVES	TWE—Teacher Wraparound Edition TCR—Teacher Classroom Resources
	📁 Blackline Master ✍ Transparency 💿 CD-ROM
	🎧 Audio Program 📼 Videocassette 🖱 Internet Resources

	OBJECTIVES
	1. In the fifteenth century, Europeans began to explore the world.
	2. Portugal, Spain, the Dutch Republic, and England reached new economic heights through worldwide trade.

	FOCUS MENU	**SUGGESTED TIME RANGES**	**SUGGESTED LEVEL**
	—— Bellringer Skillbuilder Activity, TWE, p. 407; used with Daily Focus Skills Transparency or Blackline Master 13-1, TCR ✍ 📁	5–10 minutes	L1
	—— Guide to Reading, TWE, p. 407	15–20 minutes	All levels
	—— Vocabulary Activity 13, TCR 📁	10–15 minutes	All levels
	—— Vocabulary PuzzleMaker 💿	15–20 minutes	All levels
	—— History Online Chapter 13 Overview 🖱	10–15 minutes	L1

	TEACH MENU		
	Guided Practice		
	—— Interdisciplinary Connections Activity, TWE, p. 408	10–15 minutes	L1, ELL
	—— Writing Activity, TWE, p. 409	15–20 minutes	L1
	—— Cooperative Learning Activity, TWE, p. 409	20–25 minutes	L2
	—— Critical Thinking, TWE, p. 410	10–15 minutes	L1
	—— Meeting Individual Needs, TWE, p. 410	20–25 minutes	L1, ELL
	—— Connecting Across Time, TWE, p. 413	10–15 minutes	L3
	—— Graphic Organizer Transparencies and Strategies 13, TCR ✍ 📁	20–25 minutes	All levels
	—— Cooperative Learning Activity 13, TCR 📁	20–25 minutes	All levels
	—— History Simulation 13, TCR 📁	25–30 minutes	All levels
	Independent Practice		
	—— Guided Reading Activity 13-1, TCR 📁	15–20 minutes	All levels
	—— Audio Program 🎧	15–20 minutes	All levels
	—— Linking Past and Present Activity 13, TCR 📁	15–20 minutes	L1
	—— Primary Source Reading 13, TCR 📁	20–25 minutes	L2
	—— Historical Significance Activity 13, TCR 📁	15–20 minutes	L2

	ASSESS MENU		
	Evaluate		
	—— Reading Essentials and Study Guide 13-1, TCR 📁	25–35 minutes	L1, ELL
	—— Section Quiz 13-1, TCR 📁	10–15 minutes	All levels
	Reteach		
	—— Reteaching Activity, TWE, p. 413	10–15 minutes	L1
	Enrich		
	—— Enrich, TWE, p. 411	15–20 minutes	L3

	CLOSE MENU		
	—— Close, TWE, p. 413	10–15 minutes	L2

See Optional Resources menu on page viii.

Grade _____ Class(es) _____ Date _____ M Tu W Th F

Teacher's Name _____ Date _____

Africa in an Age of Transition   Section 2 *(pp. 415–418)*

LOCAL OBJECTIVES	TWE—Teacher Wraparound Edition TCR—Teacher Classroom Resources
	📁 Blackline Master ✍ Transparency 💿 CD-ROM
	🔊 Audio Program 📼 Videocassette 🖱 Internet Resources

	OBJECTIVES **1.** European expansion affected Africa with the dramatic increase of the slave trade. **2.** Traditional political systems and cultures continued to exist in most of Africa.		
	FOCUS MENU	**SUGGESTED TIME RANGES**	**SUGGESTED LEVEL**
	—— Bellringer Skillbuilder Activity, TWE, p. 415; used with Daily Focus Skills Transparency or Blackline Master 13-2, TCR ✍ 📁	5–10 minutes	L1
	—— Guide to Reading, TWE, p. 415	15–20 minutes	All levels
	—— Vocabulary PuzzleMaker 💿	15–20 minutes	All levels
	TEACH MENU **Guided Practice**		
	—— Critical Thinking Activity, TWE, p. 416	10–15 minutes	L1
	—— History Online Student Web Activity 13 🖱		
	—— Critical Thinking, TWE, p. 417	10–15 minutes	L2
	—— Cooperative Learning Activity, TWE, p. 417	25–30 minutes	L3
	—— Graphic Organizer Transparencies and Strategies 13, TCR ✍ 📁	20–25 minutes	All levels
	Independent Practice		
	—— Guided Reading Activity 13-2, TCR 📁	15–20 minutes	L1, ELL
	—— Audio Program 🔊	20–25 minutes	All levels, ELL
	—— Critical Thinking Activity 13, TCR 📁	10–15 minutes	L1
	ASSESS MENU **Evaluate**		
	—— Reading Essentials and Study Guide 13-2, TCR 📁	25–35 minutes	L1, ELL
	—— Section Quiz 13-2, TCR 📁	10–15 minutes	All levels
	—— Interactive Tutor Self-Assessment CD-ROM, TCR 💿	20–30 minutes	All levels
	Reteach		
	—— Reteaching Activity, TWE, p. 418	10–15 minutes	L1
	Enrich		
	—— Enrich, TWE, p. 416	10–15 minutes	L1
	CLOSE MENU		
	—— Close, TWE, p. 418	10–15 minutes	L2

See Optional Resources menu on page viii.

Southeast Asia in the Era of the Spice Trade

Section 3 *(pp. 419–422)*

LOCAL OBJECTIVES	TWE—Teacher Wraparound Edition TCR—Teacher Classroom Resources 📁 Blackline Master 🖳 Transparency 💿 CD-ROM 🎧 Audio Program 📼 Videocassette ⌇ Internet Resources

	OBJECTIVES **1.** The Portuguese occupied the Moluccas in search of spices but were pushed out by the Dutch. **2.** The arrival of the Europeans greatly impacted the Malay.

	FOCUS MENU	**SUGGESTED TIME RANGES**	**SUGGESTED LEVEL**
	—— Bellringer Skillbuilder Activity, TWE, p. 419; used with Daily Focus Skills Transparency or Blackline Master 13-3, TCR 🖳 📁	5–10 minutes	L1
	—— Guide to Reading, TWE, p. 419	10–15 minutes	All levels
	—— Vocabulary PuzzleMaker 💿	15–20 minutes	All levels

	TEACH MENU **Guided Practice**		
	—— Cooperative Learning Activity, TWE, p. 420	20–25 minutes	L2
	—— Writing Activity, TWE, p. 421	15–20 minutes	L2
	—— Interdisciplinary Connections Activity, TWE, p. 421	20–25 minutes	L2
	—— Graphic Organizer Transparencies and Strategies 13, TCR 🖳 📁	20–25 minutes	All levels
	Independent Practice		
	—— Guided Reading Activity 13-3, TCR 📁	15–20 minutes	L1, ELL
	—— Skills Reinforcement Activity 13, TCR 📁	15–20 minutes	All levels
	—— Audio Program 🎧	20–25 minutes	All levels, ELL
	—— Time Line Activity 13, TCR 📁	10–15 minutes	L1

	ASSESS MENU **Evaluate**		
	—— Reading Essentials and Study Guide 13-3, TCR 📁	25–35 minutes	L1, ELL
	—— Section Quiz 13-3, TCR 📁	25–30 minutes	All levels
	—— Chapter 13 Tests, TCR 📁		
	—— Interactive Tutor Self-Assessment CD-ROM, TCR 💿	20–30 minutes	All levels
	—— MindJogger Videoquiz, Chapter 13 📼	20–25 minutes	All levels
	—— History Online Self-Check Quiz 13 ⌇	15–20 minutes	All levels
	—— Performance Assessment Activity 13, TCR 📁	20–25 minutes	All levels
	Reteach		
	—— Reteaching Activity, TWE, p. 422	15–20 minutes	L1, ELL
	—— Reteaching Activity 13, TCR 📁	15–20 minutes	L1
	Enrich		
	—— Enrich, TWE, p. 421	5–10 minutes	L1

	CLOSE MENU —— Close, TWE, p. 422	5–10 minutes	L1

See Optional Resources menu on page viii.

Europe in Crisis: The Wars of Religion Section 1 *(pp. 429–432)*

LOCAL OBJECTIVES	TWE—Teacher Wraparound Edition TCR—Teacher Classroom Resources 📁 Blackline Master ✊ Transparency 💿 CD-ROM 🔊 Audio Program 📼 Videocassette ⬤⤳ Internet Resources

	OBJECTIVES
	1. In many European nations, Protestants and Catholics fought for political and religious control.
	2. During the sixteenth and seventeenth centuries, many European rulers extended their power and their borders.

	FOCUS MENU	SUGGESTED TIME RANGES	SUGGESTED LEVEL
	—— Bellringer Skillbuilder Activity, TWE, p. 429; used with Daily Focus Skills Transparency or Blackline Master 14-1, TCR ✊ 📁	5–10 minutes	L1
	—— Guide to Reading, TWE, p. 429	15–20 minutes	All levels
	—— Vocabulary Activity 14, TCR 📁	10–15 minutes	All levels
	—— Vocabulary PuzzleMaker 💿	15–20 minutes	All levels
	—— History Online Chapter 14 Overview ⬤⤳	10–15 minutes	L1

	TEACH MENU		
	Guided Practice		
	—— Cooperative Learning Activity, TWE, p. 430	25–30 minutes	L2
	—— Critical Thinking, TWE, p. 431	5–10 minutes	L1
	—— Meeting Individual Needs, TWE, p. 431	20–25 minutes	L1
	—— Graphic Organizer Transparencies and Strategies 14, TCR ✊ 📁	20–25 minutes	All levels
	Independent Practice		
	—— Guided Reading Activity 14-1, TCR 📁	15–20 minutes	All levels
	—— Audio Program 🔊	15–20 minutes	All levels
	—— Critical Thinking Skills Activity 14, TCR 📁	10–15 minutes	L1

	ASSESS MENU		
	Evaluate		
	—— Reading Essentials and Study Guide 14-1, TCR 📁	25–35 minutes	L1, ELL
	—— Section Quiz 14-1, TCR 📁	10–15 minutes	All levels
	—— Interactive Tutor Self-Assessment CD-ROM, TCR 💿	20–30 minutes	All levels
	—— MindJogger Videoquiz, Chapter 14 📼	20–25 minutes	All levels
	Reteach		
	—— Reteaching Activity, TWE, p. 432	15–20 minutes	L1
	Enrich		
	—— Enrich, TWE, p. 430	5–10 minutes	L2
	—— Enrichment Activity 14, TCR 📁	10–15 minutes	L1

	CLOSE MENU		
	—— Close, TWE, p. 432	5–10 minutes	L2

See Optional Resources menu on page viii.

Social Crises, War, and Revolution   Section 2 *(pp. 434–439)*

LOCAL OBJECTIVES	TWE—Teacher Wraparound Edition ▭ Blackline Master ▵ Transparency ◉ CD-ROM ◑ Audio Program ▭ Videocassette ◖ Internet Resources	TCR—Teacher Classroom Resources	
	OBJECTIVES **1.** The Thirty Years' War ended the unity of the Holy Roman Empire. **2.** Democratic ideals were strengthened as a result of the English and Glorious Revolutions.		
	FOCUS MENU	**SUGGESTED TIME RANGES**	**SUGGESTED LEVEL**
	—— Bellringer Skillbuilder Activity, TWE, p. 434; used with Daily Focus Skills Transparency or Blackline Master 14-2, TCR ▵ ▭	5–10 minutes	L1
	—— Guide to Reading, TWE, p. 434	15–20 minutes	All levels
	—— Vocabulary PuzzleMaker ◉	15–20 minutes	All levels
	TEACH MENU **Guided Practice**		
	—— Critical Thinking, TWE, p. 436	20–25 minutes	L1, L2
	—— Meeting Individual Needs, TWE, p. 436	15–20 minutes	L1
	—— Writing Activity, TWE, p. 437	15–20 minutes	L2
	—— Meeting Individual Needs, TWE, p. 438	20–25 minutes	L2
	—— Graphic Organizer Transparencies and Strategies 14, TCR ▵ ▭	20–25 minutes	All levels
	Independent Practice		
	—— Guided Reading Activity 14-2, TCR ▭	15–20 minutes	L1, ELL
	—— Skills Reinforcement Activity 14, TCR ▭	15–20 minutes	All levels
	—— Audio Program ◑	20–25 minutes	All levels, ELL
	—— Historical Significance Activity 14, TCR ▭	10–15 minutes	L2
	ASSESS MENU **Evaluate**		
	—— Reading Essentials and Study Guide 14-2, TCR ▭	25–35 minutes	L1, ELL
	—— Section Quiz 14-2, TCR ▭	10–15 minutes	All levels
	—— Interactive Tutor Self-Assessment CD-ROM, TCR ◉	20–30 minutes	All levels
	Reteach		
	—— Reteaching Activity, TWE, p. 439	5–10 minutes	L1
	Enrich		
	—— Enrich, TWE, p. 435	5–10 minutes	L2
	CLOSE MENU		
	—— Close, TWE, p. 439	5–10 minutes	L1

See Optional Resources menu on page viii.

Response to Crisis: Absolutism   Section 3 *(pp. 441–447)*

LOCAL OBJECTIVES	TWE—Teacher Wraparound Edition TCR—Teacher Classroom Resources 📁 Blackline Master 🔦 Transparency 💿 CD-ROM 🎧 Audio Program 📼 Videocassette 🖱 Internet Resources

	OBJECTIVES **1.** Louis XIV was an absolute monarch whose extravagant lifestyle and military campaigns weakened France. **2.** Prussia, Austria, and Russia emerged as great European powers in the seventeenth and eighteenth centuries.		

	FOCUS MENU	**SUGGESTED TIME RANGES**	**SUGGESTED LEVEL**
	—— Bellringer Skillbuilder Activity, TWE, p. 441; used with Daily Focus Skills Transparency or Blackline Master 14-3, TCR 🔦 📁	5–10 minutes	L1
	—— Guide to Reading, TWE, p. 441	5–10 minutes	All levels
	—— Vocabulary PuzzleMaker 💿	15–20 minutes	All levels

	TEACH MENU **Guided Practice**		
	—— Critical Thinking, TWE, p. 442	5–10 minutes	L1
	—— Interdisciplinary Connections Activity, TWE, p. 442	25–30 minutes	L2
	—— Critical Thinking Activity, TWE, p. 443	20–25 minutes	L2
	—— Meeting Individual Needs, TWE, p. 444	20–25 minutes	L1, ELL
	—— Charting Activity, TWE, p. 445	10–15 minutes	L1
	—— Connecting Across Time, TWE, p. 445	5–10 minutes	L1
	—— Cooperative Learning Activity, TWE, p. 445	20–25 minutes	L2
	—— Writing Activity, TWE, p. 446	15–20 minutes	L1
	—— Graphic Organizer Transparencies and Strategies 14, TCR 🔦 📁	20–25 minutes	All levels
	—— Cooperative Learning Activity 14, TCR 📁	20–25 minutes	All levels
	—— History Simulation 14, TCR 📁	20–25 minutes	All levels
	Independent Practice		
	—— Guided Reading Activity 14-3, TCR 📁	15–20 minutes	L1, ELL
	—— Linking Past and Present Activity 14, TCR 📁	15–20 minutes	L1
	—— Primary Source Reading 14, TCR 📁	20–25 minutes	L2
	—— Time Line Activity 14, TCR 📁	10–15 minutes	L2

	ASSESS MENU **Evaluate**		
	—— Reading Essentials and Study Guide 14-3, TCR 📁	25–35 minutes	L1, ELL
	—— Section Quiz 14-3, TCR 📁	10–15 minutes	All levels
	Reteach		
	—— Reteaching Activity, TWE, p. 447	5–10 minutes	L1
	Enrich		
	—— Enrich, TWE, p. 445	10–15 minutes	L2

	CLOSE MENU		
	—— Close, TWE, p. 447	5–10 minutes	L1

See Optional Resources menu on page viii.

The World of European Culture   Section 4 *(pp. 448–451)*

LOCAL OBJECTIVES	TWE—Teacher Wraparound Edition TCR—Teacher Classroom Resources 📁 Blackline Master 🎚 Transparency 💿 CD-ROM 🎧 Audio Program 📼 Videocassette ➥ Internet Resources

OBJECTIVES

1. The artistic movements of Mannerism and the baroque began in Italy and both reflected the spiritual perceptions of the time.

2. Shakespeare and Lope de Vega were prolific writers of dramas and comedies that reflected the human condition.

FOCUS MENU	SUGGESTED TIME RANGES	SUGGESTED LEVEL
—— Bellringer Skillbuilder Activity, TWE, p. 448; used with Daily Focus Skills Transparency or Blackline Master 14-4, TCR 🎚 📁	5–10 minutes	L1
—— Guide to Reading, TWE, p. 448	10–15 minutes	All levels
—— Vocabulary PuzzleMaker 💿	15–20 minutes	All levels

TEACH MENU
Guided Practice

—— Interdisciplinary Connections Activity, TWE, p. 449	20–25 minutes	L3
—— Meeting Individual Needs, TWE, p. 450	20–25 minutes	L1
—— History Online Student Web Activity 14 ➥		
—— Graphic Organizer Transparencies and Strategies 14, TCR 🎚 📁	20–25 minutes	All levels

Independent Practice

—— Guided Reading Activity 14-4, TCR 📁	15–20 minutes	L1, ELL
—— Audio Program 🎧	20–25 minutes	All levels, ELL

ASSESS MENU
Evaluate

—— Reading Essentials and Study Guide 14-4, TCR 📁	25–35 minutes	L1, ELL
—— Section Quiz 14-4, TCR 📁	20–30 minutes	All levels
—— Chapter 14 Tests, TCR 📁		
—— Interactive Tutor Self-Assessment CD-ROM, TCR 💿	20–30 minutes	All levels
—— MindJogger Videoquiz, Chapter 14 📼	20–25 minutes	All levels
—— History Online Self-Check Quiz 14 ➥	15–20 minutes	All levels
—— Performance Assessment Activity 14, TCR 📁	20–25 minutes	All levels

Reteach

—— Reteaching Activity, TWE, p. 451	5–10 minutes	L1
—— Reteaching Activity 14, TCR 📁	15–20 minutes	L1

CLOSE MENU

—— Close, TWE, p. 451	5–10 minutes	L2

See Optional Resources menu on page viii.

The Ottoman Empire

Section 1 *(pp. 457–463)*

LOCAL OBJECTIVES	TWE—Teacher Wraparound Edition TCR—Teacher Classroom Resources 📁 Blackline Master 🖼 Transparency 💿 CD-ROM 🎧 Audio Program 📼 Videocassette ⬤⌐ Internet Resources

	OBJECTIVES
	1. Ottoman Turks used firearms to expand their lands and appointed local rulers to administer conquered regions. **2.** The Ottomans created a strong empire with religious tolerance and artistic achievements.

	FOCUS MENU	**SUGGESTED TIME RANGES**	**SUGGESTED LEVEL**
	—— Bellringer Skillbuilder Activity, TWE, p. 457; used with Daily Focus Skills Transparency or Blackline Master 15-1, TCR 🖼 📁	5–10 minutes	L1
	—— Guide to Reading, TWE, p. 457	15–20 minutes	All levels
	—— Vocabulary Activity 15, TCR 📁	10–15 minutes	All levels
	—— Vocabulary PuzzleMaker 💿	15–20 minutes	All levels
	—— History Online Chapter 15 Overview ⬤⌐	10–15 minutes	L1

	TEACH MENU		
	Guided Practice		
	—— Cooperative Learning Activity, TWE, p. 459	10–15 minutes	L1
	—— History Online Student Web Activity 15 ⬤⌐		
	—— Writing Activity, TWE, p. 460	15–20 minutes	L1
	—— Critical Thinking Activity, TWE, p. 460	10–15 minutes	L1
	—— Writing Activity, TWE, p. 461	20–25 minutes	L2
	—— Critical Thinking Activity, TWE, p. 461	20–25 minutes	L1
	—— Interdisciplinary Connections Activity, TWE, p. 462	10–15 minutes	L3
	—— Graphic Organizer Transparencies and Strategies 15, TCR 🖼 📁	20–25 minutes	All levels
	Independent Practice		
	—— Guided Reading Activity 15-1, TCR 📁	15–20 minutes	All levels
	—— Audio Program 🎧	15–20 minutes	All levels

	ASSESS MENU		
	Evaluate		
	—— Reading Essentials and Study Guide 15-1, TCR 📁	25–35 minutes	L1, ELL
	—— Section Quiz 15-1, TCR 📁	10–15 minutes	All levels
	—— Interactive Tutor Self-Assessment CD-ROM, TCR 💿	20–30 minutes	All levels
	—— MindJogger Videoquiz, Chapter 15 📼	20–25 minutes	All levels
	Reteach		
	—— Reteaching Activity, TWE, p. 463	10–15 minutes	L1
	Enrich		
	—— Enrich, TWE, p. 459	5–10 minutes	L1

	CLOSE MENU		
	—— Close, TWE, p. 463	10–15 minutes	L1

See Optional Resources menu on page viii.

The Rule of the Safavids

Section 2 *(pp. 468–471)*

LOCAL OBJECTIVES	TWE—Teacher Wraparound Edition 📁 Blackline Master 🎛 Transparency 📻 Audio Program 📼 Videocassette	TCR—Teacher Classroom Resources 💿 CD-ROM 🖊 Internet Resources
	OBJECTIVES **1.** The Safavids used their faith as a unifying force to bring Turks and Persians together. **2.** The Safavid dynasty reached its height under Shah Abbas.	

		SUGGESTED TIME RANGES	SUGGESTED LEVEL
	FOCUS MENU		
	—— Bellringer Skillbuilder Activity, TWE, p. 468; used with Daily Focus Skills Transparency or Blackline Master 15-2, TCR 🎛 📁	5–10 minutes	L1
	—— Guide to Reading, TWE, p. 468	15–20 minutes	All levels
	—— Vocabulary PuzzleMaker 💿	15–20 minutes	All levels
	TEACH MENU **Guided Practice**		
	—— Interdisciplinary Connections Activity, TWE, p. 469	10–15 minutes	L2
	—— Critical Thinking Activity, TWE, p. 470	10–15 minutes	L2
	—— Graphic Organizer Transparencies and Strategies 15, TCR 🎛 📁	20–25 minutes	All levels
	Independent Practice		
	—— Guided Reading Activity 15-2, TCR 📁	15–20 minutes	L1, ELL
	—— Skills Reinforcement Activity 15, TCR 📁	15–20 minutes	All levels
	—— Audio Program 📻	20–25 minutes	All levels, ELL
	—— Linking Past and Present Activity 15, TCR 📁	15–20 minutes	L2
	ASSESS MENU **Evaluate**		
	—— Reading Essentials and Study Guide 15-2, TCR 📁	25–35 minutes	L1, ELL
	—— Section Quiz 15-2, TCR 📁	10–15 minutes	All levels
	—— Interactive Tutor Self-Assessment CD-ROM, TCR 💿	20–30 minutes	All levels
	Reteach —— Reteaching Activity, TWE, p. 471	5–10 minutes	L1
	Enrich —— Enrich, TWE, p. 470	15–20 minutes	L1
	—— Enrichment Activity 15, TCR 📁	15–20 minutes	L3
	CLOSE MENU —— Close, TWE, p. 471	10–15 minutes	L2

See Optional Resources menu on page viii.

The Grandeur of the Moguls   Section 3 (pp. 473–478)

LOCAL OBJECTIVES	TWE—Teacher Wraparound Edition TCR—Teacher Classroom Resources 📁 Blackline Master ✋ Transparency 💿 CD-ROM 🔊 Audio Program 📼 Videocassette � Internet Resources

	OBJECTIVES **1.** The Moguls united India under a single government with a common culture. **2.** The introduction of foreigners seeking trade opportunities in India hastened the decline of the Mogul Empire.		
	FOCUS MENU	**SUGGESTED TIME RANGES**	**SUGGESTED LEVEL**
	—— Bellringer Skillbuilder Activity, TWE, p. 473; used with Daily Focus Skills Transparency or Blackline Master 15-3, TCR ✋ 📁	5–10 minutes	L1
	—— Guide to Reading, TWE, p. 473	10–15 minutes	All levels
	—— Vocabulary PuzzleMaker 💿	15–20 minutes	All levels
	TEACH MENU **Guided Practice**		
	—— Connecting Across Time, TWE, p. 476	15–20 minutes	L2
	—— Critical Thinking Activity, TWE, p. 476	20–25 minutes	L2
	—— Charting Activity, TWE, p. 477	10–15 minutes	L2
	—— Meeting Individual Needs, TWE, p. 477	20–25 minutes	L1
	—— Graphic Organizer Transparencies and Strategies 15, TCR ✋ 📁	20–25 minutes	All levels
	—— Cooperative Learning Activity 15, TCR 📁	20–25 minutes	All levels
	—— History Simulation 15, TCR 📼	30–35 minutes	All levels
	Independent Practice		
	—— Guided Reading Activity 15-3, TCR 📁	15–20 minutes	L1, ELL
	—— Primary Source Reading 15, TCR 📁	20–25 minutes	L2
	—— Historical Significance Activity 15, TCR 📁	10–15 minutes	L2
	—— Time Line Activity 15, TCR 📁	10–15 minutes	L1
	—— Critical Thinking Skills Activity 15, TCR 📁	15–20 minutes	L2
	ASSESS MENU **Evaluate**		
	—— Reading Essentials and Study Guide 15-3, TCR 📁	25–35 minutes	L1, ELL
	—— Section Quiz 15-3, TCR 📁	25–30 minutes	All levels
	—— Chapter 15 Tests, TCR 📁		
	—— History Online Self-Check Quiz 15 �	15–20 minutes	All levels
	—— Performance Assessment Activity 15, TCR 📁	15–20 minutes	All levels
	Reteach		
	—— Reteaching Activity, TWE, p. 478	10–15 minutes	L2
	—— Reteaching Activity 15, TCR 📁	15–20 minutes	L1
	Enrich		
	—— Enrich, TWE, p. 475	5–10 minutes	L1
	CLOSE MENU		
	—— Close, TWE, p. 478	5–10 minutes	L1

See Optional Resources menu on page viii.

China at Its Height

Section 1 *(pp. 485–490)*

LOCAL OBJECTIVES	TWE—Teacher Wraparound Edition TCR—Teacher Classroom Resources
	📁 Blackline Master 🖌 Transparency 🪙 CD-ROM
	🎧 Audio Program 📼 Videocassette ⟿ Internet Resources

	OBJECTIVES
	1. China opened its doors to Europeans but closed those doors when it observed the effect of Western ideas on Chinese society.
	2. Between 1500 and 1800, Chinese art and culture flourished.

	FOCUS MENU	**SUGGESTED TIME RANGES**	**SUGGESTED LEVEL**
	—— Bellringer Skillbuilder Activity, TWE, p. 485; used with Daily Focus Skills Transparency or Blackline Master 16-1, TCR 🖌 📁	5–10 minutes	L1
	—— Guide to Reading, TWE, p. 485	15–20 minutes	All levels
	—— Vocabulary Activity 16, TCR 📁	10–15 minutes	All levels
	—— Vocabulary PuzzleMaker 🪙	15–20 minutes	All levels
	—— History Online Chapter 16 Overview ⟿	10–15 minutes	L1

	TEACH MENU		
	Guided Practice		
	—— Cooperative Learning Activity, TWE, p. 486	15–20 minutes	L1
	—— Critical Thinking, TWE, p. 487	15–20 minutes	L3
	—— Cooperative Learning Activity, TWE, p. 487	25–30 minutes	L3
	—— Cooperative Learning Activity, TWE, p. 488	20–25 minutes	L2
	—— Critical Thinking, TWE, p. 489	10–15 minutes	L2
	—— Critical Thinking, TWE, p. 490	10–15 minutes	L3
	—— Graphic Organizer Transparencies and Strategies 16, TCR 🖌 📁	20–25 minutes	All levels
	Independent Practice		
	—— Guided Reading Activity 16-1, TCR 📁	15–20 minutes	All levels
	—— Audio Program 🎧	15–20 minutes	All levels

	ASSESS MENU		
	Evaluate		
	—— Reading Essentials and Study Guide 16-1, TCR 📁	25–35 minutes	L1, ELL
	—— Section Quiz 16-1, TCR 📁	10–15 minutes	All levels
	—— Interactive Tutor Self-Assessment CD-ROM, TCR 🪙	20–30 minutes	All levels
	—— MindJogger Videoquiz, Chapter 16 📼	20–25 minutes	All levels
	Reteach		
	—— Reteaching Activity, TWE, p. 489	15–20 minutes	L1
	Enrich		
	—— Enrich, TWE, p. 486	25–30 minutes	L2
	—— Enrichment Activity 16, TCR 📁	10–15 minutes	L2

	CLOSE MENU		
	—— Close, TWE, p. 490	5–10 minutes	L1

See Optional Resources menu on page viii.

Chinese Society and Culture Section 2 *(pp. 491–494)*

LOCAL OBJECTIVES	TWE—Teacher Wraparound Edition TCR—Teacher Classroom Resources
	🗀 Blackline Master 🖬 Transparency 💿 CD-ROM
	🎧 Audio Program 📼 Videocassette 🖱 Internet Resources

	OBJECTIVES **1.** A rapid increase in population led to rural land shortages. **2.** Chinese society was organized around the family. **3.** Architecture, decorative arts, and literature flourished during this period.		
	FOCUS MENU	**SUGGESTED TIME RANGES**	**SUGGESTED LEVEL**
	—— Bellringer Skillbuilder Activity, TWE, p. 491; used with Daily Focus Skills Transparency or Blackline Master 16-2, TCR 🖬 🗀	5–10 minutes	L1
	—— Guide to Reading, TWE, p. 491	15–20 minutes	All levels
	—— Vocabulary PuzzleMaker 💿	15–20 minutes	All levels
	TEACH MENU **Guided Practice**		
	—— Cooperative Learning Activity, TWE, p. 492	15–20 minutes	L2
	—— Meeting Individual Needs, TWE, p. 493	20–25 minutes	L2
	—— Graphic Organizer Transparencies and Strategies 16, TCR 🖬 🗀	20–25 minutes	All levels
	Independent Practice		
	—— Guided Reading Activity 16-2, TCR 🗀	15–20 minutes	L1, ELL
	—— Skills Reinforcement Activity 16, TCR 🗀	15–20 minutes	All levels
	—— Audio Program 🎧	20–25 minutes	All levels, ELL
	—— Linking Past and Present Activity 16, TCR 🗀	15–20 minutes	L2
	ASSESS MENU **Evaluate**		
	—— Reading Essentials and Study Guide 16-2, TCR 🗀	25–35 minutes	L1, ELL
	—— Section Quiz 16-2, TCR 🗀	10–15 minutes	All levels
	—— Interactive Tutor Self-Assessment CD-ROM, TCR 💿	20–30 minutes	All levels
	Reteach —— Reteaching Activity, TWE, p. 494	5–10 minutes	L1
	CLOSE MENU —— Close, TWE, p. 494	10–15 minutes	L1

See Optional Resources menu on page viii.

Grade _____ Class(es) _____ Date _____ M Tu W Th F

Teacher's Name _____ Date _____

Tokugawa Japan and Korea   Section 3 *(pp. 496–500)*

LOCAL OBJECTIVES	TWE—Teacher Wraparound Edition TCR—Teacher Classroom Resources
	📁 Blackline Master 🖋 Transparency 💿 CD-ROM
	🎧 Audio Program 📼 Videocassette 🔌 Internet Resources

	OBJECTIVES **1.** Japan was unified by three powerful political figures. **2.** Between 1500 and 1800, Japan experienced many peasant uprisings. **3.** Korea could not withstand invasions by the Japanese and Manchus.

		SUGGESTED TIME RANGES	SUGGESTED LEVEL
	FOCUS MENU		
	—— Bellringer Skillbuilder Activity, TWE, p. 496; used with Daily Focus Skills Transparency or Blackline Master 16-3, TCR 🖋 📁	5–10 minutes	L1
	—— Guide to Reading, TWE, p. 496	10–15 minutes	All levels
	—— Vocabulary PuzzleMaker 💿	15–20 minutes	All levels
	TEACH MENU		
	Guided Practice		
	—— History Online Student Web Activity 16 🔌		
	—— Cooperative Learning Activity, TWE, p. 497	25–30 minutes	L2
	—— Connecting Across Time, TWE, p. 499	5–10 minutes	L1
	—— Critical Thinking, TWE, p. 500	10–15 minutes	L1
	—— Graphic Organizer Transparencies and Strategies 16, TCR 🖋 📁	20–25 minutes	All levels
	—— Cooperative Learning Activity 16, TCR 📁	20–25 minutes	All levels
	—— History Simulation 16, TCR 📁	30–35 minutes	All levels
	Independent Practice		
	—— Guided Reading Activity 16-3, TCR 📁	15–20 minutes	L1, ELL
	—— Audio Program 🎧	20–25 minutes	All levels, ELL
	—— Primary Source Reading 16, TCR 📁	20–25 minutes	L3
	—— Historical Significance Activity 16, TCR 📁	15–20 minutes	L3
	—— Time Line Activity 16, TCR 📁	10–15 minutes	L1
	—— Critical Thinking Skills Activity 16, TCR 📁	10–15 minutes	L2
	ASSESS MENU		
	Evaluate		
	—— Reading Essentials and Study Guide 16-3, TCR 📁	25–35 minutes	L1, ELL
	—— Section Quiz 16-3, TCR 📁	25–30 minutes	All levels
	—— Chapter 16 Tests, TCR 📁		
	—— Interactive Tutor Self-Assessment CD-ROM, TCR 💿	20–30 minutes	All levels
	—— MindJogger Videoquiz, Chapter 16 📼	20–25 minutes	All levels
	—— History Online Self-Check Quiz 16 🔌	15–20 minutes	All levels
	—— Performance Assessment Activity 16, TCR 📁	15–20 minutes	All levels
	Reteach		
	—— Reteaching Activity, TWE, p. 499	10–15 minutes	L1
	—— Reteaching Activity 16, TCR 📁	15–20 minutes	L1
	CLOSE MENU		
	—— Close, TWE, p. 500	5–10 minutes	L1

See Optional Resources menu on page viii.

The Scientific Revolution

Section 1 *(pp. 511–517)*

LOCAL OBJECTIVES	TWE—Teacher Wraparound Edition TCR—Teacher Classroom Resources 🗁 Blackline Master ♟ Transparency 💿 CD-ROM 📢 Audio Program 📼 Videocassette ⬤⫘ Internet Resources

OBJECTIVE

The Scientific Revolution gave Europeans a new way to view humankind's place in the universe.

	FOCUS MENU	**SUGGESTED TIME RANGES**	**SUGGESTED LEVEL**
	—— Bellringer Skillbuilder Activity, TWE, p. 511; used with Daily Focus Skills Transparency or Blackline Master 17-1, TCR ♟ 🗁	5–10 minutes	L1
	—— Guide to Reading, TWE, p. 511	15–20 minutes	All levels
	—— Vocabulary Activity 17, TCR 🗁	10–15 minutes	All levels
	—— Vocabulary PuzzleMaker 💿	15–20 minutes	All levels
	—— History Online Chapter 17 Overview ⬤⫘	10–15 minutes	L1
	TEACH MENU **Guided Practice**		
	—— Cooperative Learning Activity, TWE, p. 513	30–35 minutes	L3
	—— Critical Thinking, TWE, p. 515	5–10 minutes	L2
	—— Critical Thinking Activity, TWE, p. 515	15–20 minutes	L3
	—— Meeting Individual Needs, TWE, p. 516	20–25 minutes	L1, ELL
	—— Graphic Organizer Transparencies and Strategies 17, TCR ♟ 🗁	20–25 minutes	All levels
	—— History Simulation 17, TCR 🗁	30–35 minutes	All levels
	Independent Practice		
	—— Guided Reading Activity 17-1, TCR 🗁	15–20 minutes	All levels
	—— Audio Program 📢	15–20 minutes	All levels
	—— Linking Past and Present Activity 17, TCR 🗁	15–20 minutes	L2
	ASSESS MENU **Evaluate**		
	—— Reading Essentials and Study Guide 17-1, TCR 🗁	25–35 minutes	L1, ELL
	—— Section Quiz 17-1, TCR 🗁	10–15 minutes	All levels
	—— Interactive Tutor Self-Assessment CD-ROM, TCR 💿	20–30 minutes	All levels
	—— MindJogger Videoquiz, Chapter 17 📼	20–25 minutes	All levels
	Reteach		
	—— Reteaching Activity, TWE, p. 517	5–10 minutes	L1, ELL
	Enrich		
	—— Enrich, TWE, p. 513	15–20 minutes	L3
	—— Enrichment Activity 17, TCR 🗁	15–20 minutes	L2
	CLOSE MENU		
	—— Close, TWE, p. 517	10–15 minutes	L2

See Optional Resources menu on page viii.

The Enlightenment

Section 2 *(pp. 518–525)*

LOCAL OBJECTIVES	TWE—Teacher Wraparound Edition TCR—Teacher Classroom Resources 📁 Blackline Master 🕹 Transparency 💿 CD-ROM 🎧 Audio Program 📼 Videocassette 🖱 Internet Resources		
	OBJECTIVES **1.** Eighteenth-century intellectuals used the ideas of the Scientific Revolution to reexamine all aspects of life. **2.** People gathered in salons to discuss the ideas of the philosophes.		
	FOCUS MENU	**SUGGESTED TIME RANGES**	**SUGGESTED LEVEL**
	—— Bellringer Skillbuilder Activity, TWE, p. 518; used with Daily Focus Skills Transparency or Blackline Master 17-2, TCR 🕹 📁	5–10 minutes	L1
	—— Guide to Reading, TWE, p. 518	15–20 minutes	All levels
	—— Vocabulary PuzzleMaker 💿	15–20 minutes	All levels
	TEACH MENU **Guided Practice**		
	—— Critical Thinking Activity, TWE, p. 519	15–20 minutes	L3
	—— Critical Thinking, TWE, p. 520	10–15 minutes	L2
	—— Writing Activity, TWE, p. 520	20–25 minutes	L2
	—— Critical Thinking, TWE, p. 521	5–10 minutes	L2
	—— Interdisciplinary Connections Activity, TWE, p. 521	20–25 minutes	L2
	—— Connecting Across Time, TWE, p. 522	10–15 minutes	L1
	—— Cooperative Learning Activity, TWE, p. 522	30–35 minutes	L1, L2
	—— Connecting Across Time, TWE, p. 523	10–15 minutes	L2
	—— Critical Thinking, TWE, p. 523	20–25 minutes	L2
	—— Graphic Organizer Transparencies and Strategies 17, TCR 🕹 📁	20–25 minutes	All levels
	Independent Practice		
	—— Guided Reading Activity 17-2, TCR 📁	15–20 minutes	L1, ELL
	—— Audio Program 🎧	20–25 minutes	All levels, ELL
	—— Primary Source Reading 17, TCR 📁	20–25 minutes	L2
	—— Historical Significance Activity 17, TCR 📁	10–15 minutes	L2
	—— Critical Thinking Skills Activity 17, TCR 📁	15–20 minutes	L2
	ASSESS MENU **Evaluate**		
	—— Reading Essentials and Study Guide 17-2, TCR 📁	25–35 minutes	L1, ELL
	—— Section Quiz 17-2, TCR 📁	10–15 minutes	All levels
	Reteach		
	—— Reteaching Activity, TWE, p. 525	5–10 minutes	L1
	Enrich		
	—— Enrich, TWE, p. 522	10–15 minutes	L3
	CLOSE MENU		
	—— Close, TWE, p. 525	15–20 minutes	L2

See Optional Resources menu on page viii.

The Impact of the Enlightenment   Section 3 *(pp. 526–534)*

LOCAL OBJECTIVES	TWE—Teacher Wraparound Edition TCR—Teacher Classroom Resources 📁 Blackline Master 🖋 Transparency ⊙ CD-ROM 🎧 Audio Program 📼 Videocassette ⌐⌐ Internet Resources		
	OBJECTIVES **1.** Enlightenment beliefs were reflected in the art, music, and literature of the time. **2.** Enlightenment thought impacted the politics of Europe in the eighteenth century.		
	FOCUS MENU	**SUGGESTED TIME RANGES**	**SUGGESTED LEVEL**
	—— Bellringer Skillbuilder Activity, TWE, p. 526; used with Daily Focus Skills Transparency or Blackline Master 17-3, TCR 🖋 📁	5–10 minutes	L1
	—— Guide to Reading, TWE, p. 526	5–10 minutes	All levels
	—— Vocabulary PuzzleMaker ⊙	15–20 minutes	All levels
	TEACH MENU **Guided Practice**		
	—— History Online Student Web Activity 17 ⌐⌐		
	—— Meeting Individual Needs, TWE, p. 527	20–25 minutes	L2
	—— Connecting Across Time, TWE, p. 528	10–15 minutes	L2
	—— Interdisciplinary Connections Activity, TWE, p. 528	25–30 minutes	L2, L3
	—— Critical Thinking, TWE, p. 529	5–10 minutes	L1
	—— Critical Thinking Activity, TWE, p. 529	20–25 minutes	L1, ELL
	—— Critical Thinking, TWE, p. 530	10–15 minutes	L3
	—— Connecting Across Time, TWE, p. 531	10–15 minutes	L2
	—— Writing Activity, TWE, p. 531	20–25 minutes	L2
	—— Charting Activity, TWE, p. 532	10–15 minutes	L1
	—— Cooperative Learning Activity, TWE, p. 532	30–35 minutes	L2
	—— Writing Activity, TWE, p. 533	25–30 minutes	L2
	—— Graphic Organizer Transparencies and Strategies 17, TCR 🖋 📁	20–25 minutes	All levels
	—— Cooperative Learning Activity 17, TCR 📁	20–25 minutes	All levels
	Independent Practice		
	—— Guided Reading Activity 17-3, TCR 📁	15–20 minutes	L1, ELL
	—— Skills Reinforcement Activity 17, TCR 📁	15–20 minutes	All levels
	—— Audio Program 🎧	20–25 minutes	All levels, ELL
	ASSESS MENU **Evaluate**		
	—— Reading Essentials and Study Guide 17-3, TCR 📁	25–35 minutes	L1, ELL
	—— Section Quiz 17-3, TCR 📁	10–15 minutes	All levels
	—— Interactive Tutor Self-Assessment CD-ROM, TCR ⊙	20–30 minutes	All levels
	—— Performance Assessment Activity 17, TCR 📁	15–20 minutes	All levels
	Reteach —— Reteaching Activity, TWE, p. 534	10–15 minutes	L1, ELL
	CLOSE MENU —— Close, TWE, p. 534	5–10 minutes	L2

See Optional Resources menu on page viii.

Colonial Empires and the American Revolution

Section 4 *(pp. 536–540)*

LOCAL OBJECTIVES	TWE—Teacher Wraparound Edition TCR—Teacher Classroom Resources
	📁 Blackline Master 🖋 Transparency 💿 CD-ROM
	🎧 Audio Program 📼 Videocassette 🖱 Internet Resources

	OBJECTIVES **1.** The colonies of Latin America and British North America were developing in ways that differed from their European mother countries. **2.** The American colonies revolted against Great Britain and formed a new nation.

		SUGGESTED TIME RANGES	SUGGESTED LEVEL
	FOCUS MENU		
	—— Bellringer Skillbuilder Activity, TWE, p. 536; used with Daily Focus Skills Transparency or Blackline Master 17-4, TCR 🖋 📁	5–10 minutes	L1
	—— Guide to Reading, TWE, p. 536	10–15 minutes	All levels
	—— Vocabulary PuzzleMaker 💿	15–20 minutes	All levels
	TEACH MENU **Guided Practice**		
	—— Critical Thinking, TWE, p. 537	10–15 minutes	L1
	—— Cooperative Learning Activity, TWE, p. 537	30–35 minutes	L1
	—— Writing Activity, TWE, p. 538	20–25 minutes	L1, L2
	—— Charting Activity, TWE, p. 539	10–15 minutes	L3
	—— Critical Thinking Activity, TWE, p. 539	10–15 minutes	L2, L3
	—— Graphic Organizer Transparencies and Strategies 17, TCR 🖋 📁	20–25 minutes	All levels
	Independent Practice		
	—— Guided Reading Activity 17-4, TCR 📁	15–20 minutes	L1, ELL
	—— Audio Program 🎧	20–25 minutes	All levels, ELL
	—— Time Line Activity 17, TCR 📁	10–15 minutes	L2
	ASSESS MENU **Evaluate**		
	—— Reading Essentials and Study Guide 17-4, TCR 📁	25–35 minutes	L1, ELL
	—— Section Quiz 17-4, TCR 📁	25–30 minutes	All levels
	—— Chapter 17 Tests, TCR 📁		
	—— Interactive Tutor Self-Assessment CD-ROM, TCR 💿	20–30 minutes	All levels
	—— MindJogger Videoquiz, Chapter 17 📼	20–25 minutes	All levels
	—— History Online Self-Check Quiz 17 🖱	15–20 minutes	All levels
	Reteach		
	—— Reteaching Activity, TWE, p. 540	10–15 minutes	L1, ELL
	—— Reteaching Activity 17, TCR 📁	15–20 minutes	L1
	Enrich		
	—— Enrich, TWE, p. 538	10–15 minutes	L2
	CLOSE MENU		
	—— Close, TWE, p. 540	10–15 minutes	L2

See Optional Resources menu on page viii.

The French Revolution Begins   Section 1 (*pp. 547–553*)

LOCAL OBJECTIVES	TWE—Teacher Wraparound Edition TCR—Teacher Classroom Resources 📁 Blackline Master 🗲 Transparency 💿 CD-ROM 🔊 Audio Program 📼 Videocassette ⌐ Internet Resources

	OBJECTIVES **1.** Social inequality and economic problems contributed to the French Revolution. **2.** Radicals, Catholic priests, nobles, and the lower classes opposed the new order.		

	FOCUS MENU	**SUGGESTED TIME RANGES**	**SUGGESTED LEVEL**
	—— Bellringer Skillbuilder Activity, TWE, p. 547; used with Daily Focus Skills Transparency or Blackline Master 18-1, TCR 🗲 📁	5–10 minutes	L1
	—— Guide to Reading, TWE, p. 547	15–20 minutes	All levels
	—— Vocabulary Activity 18, TCR 📁	10–15 minutes	All levels
	—— Vocabulary PuzzleMaker 💿	15–20 minutes	All levels
	—— History Online Chapter 18 Overview ⌐	10–15 minutes	L1

	TEACH MENU **Guided Practice**		
	—— Interdisciplinary Connections Activity, TWE, p. 548	25–30 minutes	L2
	—— Connecting Across Time, TWE, p. 549	10–15 minutes	L2
	—— Cooperative Learning Activity, TWE, p. 549	20–25 minutes	L3
	—— Meeting Individual Needs, TWE, p. 550	20–25 minutes	L2
	—— Writing Activity, TWE, p. 551	20–25 minutes	L2
	—— Graphic Organizer Transparencies and Strategies 18, TCR 🗲 📁	20–25 minutes	All levels
	—— History Simulation 18, TCR 📁	20–25 minutes	All levels
	Independent Practice		
	—— Guided Reading Activity 18-1, TCR 📁	15–20 minutes	All levels
	—— Audio Program 🔊	15–20 minutes	All levels
	—— Linking Past and Present Activity 18, TCR 📁	15–20 minutes	L3
	—— Primary Source Reading 18, TCR 📁	20–25 minutes	L3
	—— Critical Thinking Skills Activity 18, TCR 📁	15–20 minutes	L2

	ASSESS MENU **Evaluate**		
	—— Reading Essentials and Study Guide 18-1, TCR 📁	25–35 minutes	L1, ELL
	—— Section Quiz 18-1, TCR 📁	10–15 minutes	All levels
	—— Interactive Tutor Self-Assessment CD-ROM, TCR 💿	20–30 minutes	All levels
	—— MindJogger Videoquiz, Chapter 18 📼	20–25 minutes	All levels
	—— Performance Assessment Activity 18, TCR 📁	15–20 minutes	All levels
	Reteach		
	—— Reteaching Activity, TWE, p. 553	15–20 minutes	L2
	Enrich		
	—— Enrich, TWE, p. 551	5–10 minutes	L1

	CLOSE MENU		
	—— Close, TWE, p. 553	5–10 minutes	L1

See Optional Resources menu on page viii.

Grade _____ Class(es) _____ Date _____ M Tu W Th F

Teacher's Name _____ Date _____

Radical Revolution and Reaction   Section 2 *(pp. 555–561)*

<table>
<tr>
<td rowspan="2">LOCAL
OBJECTIVES</td>
<td colspan="3">TWE—Teacher Wraparound Edition   TCR—Teacher Classroom Resources
📁 Blackline Master   📠 Transparency   💿 CD-ROM
🎧 Audio Program   📼 Videocassette   🖱 Internet Resources</td>
</tr>
<tr>
<td colspan="3">OBJECTIVES
1. Radical groups and leaders controlled the Revolution.
2. The new French Republic faced enemies at home and abroad.</td>
</tr>
<tr>
<td></td>
<td>FOCUS MENU</td>
<td>SUGGESTED
TIME RANGES</td>
<td>SUGGESTED
LEVEL</td>
</tr>
<tr>
<td></td>
<td>—— Bellringer Skillbuilder Activity, TWE,
    p. 555; used with Daily Focus Skills
    Transparency or Blackline Master 18-2, TCR 📠 📁</td>
<td>5–10 minutes</td>
<td>L1</td>
</tr>
<tr>
<td></td>
<td>—— Guide to Reading, TWE, p. 555</td>
<td>15–20 minutes</td>
<td>All levels</td>
</tr>
<tr>
<td></td>
<td>—— Vocabulary PuzzleMaker 💿</td>
<td>15–20 minutes</td>
<td>All levels</td>
</tr>
<tr>
<td></td>
<td>TEACH MENU
Guided Practice
—— Cooperative Learning Activity, TWE, p. 556</td>
<td>25–30 minutes</td>
<td>L2</td>
</tr>
<tr>
<td></td>
<td>—— Connecting Across Time, TWE, p. 557</td>
<td>10–15 minutes</td>
<td>L3</td>
</tr>
<tr>
<td></td>
<td>—— Critical Thinking, TWE, p. 558</td>
<td>5–10 minutes</td>
<td>L3</td>
</tr>
<tr>
<td></td>
<td>—— Writing Activity, TWE, p. 558</td>
<td>20–25 minutes</td>
<td>L2</td>
</tr>
<tr>
<td></td>
<td>—— Interdisciplinary Connections Activity, TWE, p. 558</td>
<td>15–20 minutes</td>
<td>L3</td>
</tr>
<tr>
<td></td>
<td>—— Writing Activity, TWE, p. 559</td>
<td>15–20 minutes</td>
<td>L2</td>
</tr>
<tr>
<td></td>
<td>—— Critical Thinking Activity, TWE, p. 559</td>
<td>20–25 minutes</td>
<td>L1</td>
</tr>
<tr>
<td></td>
<td>—— Critical Thinking Activity, TWE, p. 560</td>
<td>15–20 minutes</td>
<td>L2</td>
</tr>
<tr>
<td></td>
<td>—— Graphic Organizer
    Transparencies and Strategies 18, TCR 📠 📁</td>
<td>20–25 minutes</td>
<td>All levels</td>
</tr>
<tr>
<td></td>
<td>Independent Practice
—— Guided Reading Activity 18-2, TCR 📁</td>
<td>15–20 minutes</td>
<td>L1, ELL</td>
</tr>
<tr>
<td></td>
<td>—— Skills Reinforcement Activity 18, TCR 📁</td>
<td>15–20 minutes</td>
<td>All levels</td>
</tr>
<tr>
<td></td>
<td>—— Audio Program 🎧</td>
<td>20–25 minutes</td>
<td>All levels, ELL</td>
</tr>
<tr>
<td></td>
<td>ASSESS MENU
Evaluate
—— Reading Essentials and Study Guide 18-2, TCR 📁</td>
<td>25–35 minutes</td>
<td>L1, ELL</td>
</tr>
<tr>
<td></td>
<td>—— Section Quiz 18-2, TCR 📁</td>
<td>10–15 minutes</td>
<td>All levels</td>
</tr>
<tr>
<td></td>
<td>—— Interactive Tutor Self-Assessment CD-ROM, TCR 💿</td>
<td>20–30 minutes</td>
<td>All levels</td>
</tr>
<tr>
<td></td>
<td>Reteach
—— Reteaching Activity, TWE, p. 561</td>
<td>5–10 minutes</td>
<td>L1</td>
</tr>
<tr>
<td></td>
<td>Enrich
—— Enrich, TWE, p. 558</td>
<td>15–20 minutes</td>
<td>L1</td>
</tr>
<tr>
<td></td>
<td>—— Enrichment Activity 18, TCR 📁</td>
<td>10–15 minutes</td>
<td>L1</td>
</tr>
<tr>
<td></td>
<td>CLOSE MENU
—— Close, TWE, p. 561</td>
<td>10–15 minutes</td>
<td>L2</td>
</tr>
</table>

See Optional Resources menu on page viii.

Grade _____ Class(es) _____ Date _____ M Tu W Th F

Teacher's Name _____ Date _____

The Age of Napoleon   Section 3 *(pp. 563–569)*

LOCAL OBJECTIVES	TWE—Teacher Wraparound Edition TCR—Teacher Classroom Resources 📁 Blackline Master ✇ Transparency ⊚ CD-ROM 🔊 Audio Program 📼 Videocassette ⬤⁻ Internet Resources

	OBJECTIVES **1.** Napoleon built and lost an empire. **2.** Nationalism spread as a result of the French Revolution. **3.** Napoleon was exiled first to Elba, and then to St. Helena, where he died.

	FOCUS MENU	**SUGGESTED TIME RANGES**	**SUGGESTED LEVEL**
	—— Bellringer Skillbuilder Activity, TWE, p. 563; used with Daily Focus Skills Transparency or Blackline Master 18-3, TCR ✇ 📁	5–10 minutes	L1
	—— Guide to Reading, TWE, p. 563	10–15 minutes	All levels
	—— Vocabulary PuzzleMaker ⊚	15–20 minutes	All levels

	TEACH MENU **Guided Practice**		
	—— Writing Activity, TWE, p. 565	25–30 minutes	L3
	—— Cooperative Learning Activity, TWE, p. 565	25–30 minutes	L2, L3
	—— Charting Activity, TWE, p. 566	10–15 minutes	L1
	—— Meeting Individual Needs, TWE, p. 566	25–30 minutes	L1, ELL
	—— Critical Thinking, TWE, p. 567	10–15 minutes	L3
	—— History Online Student Web Activity 18 ⬤⁻		
	—— Writing Activity, TWE, p. 568	15–20 minutes	L2, ELL
	—— Interdisciplinary Connections Activity, TWE, p. 568	25–30 minutes	L1, ELL
	—— Cooperative Learning Activity 18, TCR 📁	20–25 minutes	All levels
	Independent Practice		
	—— Guided Reading Activity 18-3, TCR 📁	15–20 minutes	L1, ELL
	—— Historical Significance Activity 18, TCR 📁	10–15 minutes	L2
	—— Time Line Activity 18, TCR 📁	10–15 minutes	L2

	ASSESS MENU **Evaluate**		
	—— Reading Essentials and Study Guide 18-3, TCR 📁	25–35 minutes	L1, ELL
	—— Section Quiz 18-3, TCR 📁	25–30 minutes	All levels
	—— Chapter 18 Tests, TCR 📁		
	—— MindJogger Videoquiz, Chapter 18 📼	20–25 minutes	All levels
	—— History Online Self-Check Quiz 18 ⬤⁻	15–20 minutes	All levels
	Reteach		
	—— Reteaching Activity, TWE, p. 569	5–10 minutes	L1, ELL
	—— Reteaching Activity 18, TCR 📁	15–20 minutes	L1
	Enrich		
	—— Enrich, TWE, p. 565	10–15 minutes	L1

	CLOSE MENU		
	—— Close, TWE, p. 569	5–10 minutes	L1

See Optional Resources menu on page viii.

The Industrial Revolution

Section 1 (pp. 581–588)

LOCAL OBJECTIVES	TWE—Teacher Wraparound Edition TCR—Teacher Classroom Resources 🗀 Blackline Master 🖎 Transparency 💿 CD-ROM 🎧 Audio Program 📼 Videocassette ⬤ᶳ Internet Resources

	OBJECTIVES **1.** Coal and steam replaced wind and water as new sources of energy and power. **2.** Cities grew as people moved from the country to work in factories.

	FOCUS MENU	**SUGGESTED TIME RANGES**	**SUGGESTED LEVEL**
	—— Bellringer Skillbuilder Activity, TWE, p. 581; used with Daily Focus Skills Transparency or Blackline Master 19-1, TCR 🖎 🗀	5–10 minutes	L1
	—— Guide to Reading, TWE, p. 581	15–20 minutes	All levels
	—— Vocabulary Activity 19, TCR 🗀	10–15 minutes	All levels
	—— Vocabulary PuzzleMaker 💿	15–20 minutes	All levels
	—— History Online Chapter 19 Overview ⬤ᶳ	10–15 minutes	L1

	TEACH MENU **Guided Practice**		
	—— Meeting Individual Needs, TWE, p. 582	10–15 minutes	L2
	—— Cooperative Learning Activity, TWE, p. 583	25–30 minutes	L2
	—— Connecting Across Time, TWE, p. 585	10–15 minutes	L1
	—— Interdisciplinary Connections Activity, TWE, p. 585	30–35 minutes	L2
	—— Meeting Individual Needs, TWE, p. 586	15–20 minutes	L1
	—— Critical Thinking Activity, TWE, p. 587	15–20 minutes	L2
	—— Graphic Organizer Transparencies and Strategies 19, TCR 🖎 🗀	20–25 minutes	All levels
	—— Cooperative Learning Activity 19, TCR 🗀	20–25 minutes	All levels
	Independent Practice		
	—— Guided Reading Activity 19-1, TCR 🗀	15–20 minutes	All levels
	—— Audio Program 🎧	15–20 minutes	All levels
	—— Primary Source Reading 19, TCR 🗀	20–25 minutes	L2
	—— Historical Significance Activity 19, TCR 🗀	10–15 minutes	L2
	—— Critical Thinking Skills Activity 19, TCR 🗀	10–15 minutes	L1

	ASSESS MENU **Evaluate**		
	—— Reading Essentials and Study Guide 19-1, TCR 🗀	25–35 minutes	L1, ELL
	—— Section Quiz 19-1, TCR 🗀	10–15 minutes	All levels
	—— Performance Assessment Activity 19, TCR 🗀	20–25 minutes	All levels
	Reteach —— Reteaching Activity, TWE, p. 588	10–15 minutes	L2
	Enrich —— Enrichment Activity 19, TCR 🗀	10–15 minutes	L1

	CLOSE MENU —— Close, TWE, p. 588	10–15 minutes	L2

See Optional Resources menu on page viii.

Grade ______________ Class(es) ______________ Date ______________ M Tu W Th F

Teacher's Name ____ Date ______________

Reaction and Revolution

Section 2 *(pp. 589–594)*

LOCAL OBJECTIVES	TWE—Teacher Wraparound Edition; TCR—Teacher Classroom Resources; Blackline Master; Transparency; CD-ROM; Audio Program; Videocassette; Internet Resources		
	OBJECTIVES **1.** The great powers worked to maintain a conservative order throughout Europe. **2.** The forces of liberalism and nationalism continued to grow and led to the revolutions of 1848.		
	FOCUS MENU	**SUGGESTED TIME RANGES**	**SUGGESTED LEVEL**
	—— Bellringer Skillbuilder Activity, TWE, p. 589; used with Daily Focus Skills Transparency or Blackline Master 19-2, TCR	5–10 minutes	L1
	—— Guide to Reading, TWE, p. 589	15–20 minutes	All levels
	—— Vocabulary PuzzleMaker	15–20 minutes	All levels
	TEACH MENU		
	Guided Practice		
	—— Meeting Individual Needs, TWE, p. 590	15–20 minutes	L1
	—— Critical Thinking, TWE, p. 591	25–30 minutes	L3
	—— Critical Thinking, TWE, p. 591	10–15 minutes	L3
	—— Critical Thinking Activity, TWE, p. 591	15–20 minutes	L2
	—— Critical Thinking, TWE, p. 592	5–10 minutes	L1
	—— Connecting Across Time, TWE, p. 592	10–15 minutes	L1
	—— Cooperative Learning Activity, TWE, p. 592	30–35 minutes	L2
	—— Writing Activity, TWE, p. 593	10–15 minutes	L3
	—— Critical Thinking, TWE, p. 593	10–15 minutes	L1
	—— Meeting Individual Needs, TWE, p. 593	10–15 minutes	L1
	—— Graphic Organizer Transparencies and Strategies 19, TCR	20–25 minutes	All levels
	Independent Practice		
	—— Guided Reading Activity 19-2, TCR	15–20 minutes	L1, ELL
	—— Audio Program	20–25 minutes	All levels, ELL
	ASSESS MENU		
	Evaluate		
	—— Reading Essentials and Study Guide 19-2, TCR	25–35 minutes	L1, ELL
	—— Section Quiz 19-2, TCR	10–15 minutes	All levels
	—— Interactive Tutor Self-Assessment CD-ROM, TCR	20–30 minutes	All levels
	Reteach		
	—— Reteaching Activity, TWE, p. 594	10–15 minutes	L1
	Enrich		
	—— Enrich, TWE, p. 592	5–10 minutes	L2
	CLOSE MENU		
	—— Close, TWE, p. 594	10–15 minutes	L2

See Optional Resources menu on page viii.

National Unification and the National State

Section 3 *(pp. 596–603)*

LOCAL OBJECTIVES	TWE—Teacher Wraparound Edition 📁 Blackline Master ✊ Transparency 🎧 Audio Program 📼 Videocassette	TCR—Teacher Classroom Resources 💿 CD-ROM 🖱 Internet Resources

	OBJECTIVES **1.** The rise of nationalism contributed to the unification of Italy and Germany. **2.** While nationalism had great appeal, not all peoples achieved the goal of establishing their own national states.		

	FOCUS MENU	**SUGGESTED TIME RANGES**	**SUGGESTED LEVEL**
	—— Bellringer Skillbuilder Activity, TWE, p. 596; used with Daily Focus Skills Transparency or Blackline Master 19-3, TCR ✊ 📁	5–10 minutes	L1
	—— Guide to Reading, TWE, p. 596	5–10 minutes	All levels
	—— Vocabulary PuzzleMaker 💿	15–20 minutes	All levels

	TEACH MENU		
	Guided Practice		
	—— Charting Activity, TWE, p. 598	15–20 minutes	L2, ELL
	—— Cooperative Learning Activity, TWE, p. 598	30–35 minutes	L2
	—— History Online Student Web Activity 19 🖱		
	—— Writing Activity, TWE, p. 600	20–25 minutes	L2
	—— Meeting Individual Needs, TWE, p. 600	20–25 minutes	L1
	—— Critical Thinking, TWE, p. 601	5–10 minutes	L2
	—— Interdisciplinary Connections Activity, TWE, p. 601	25–30 minutes	L3
	—— Cooperative Learning Activity, TWE, p. 602	25–30 minutes	L1
	—— Graphic Organizer Transparencies and Strategies 19, TCR ✊ 📁	20–25 minutes	All levels
	Independent Practice		
	—— Guided Reading Activity 19-3, TCR 📁	15–20 minutes	L1, ELL
	—— Skills Reinforcement Activity 19, TCR 📁	15–20 minutes	All levels
	—— Audio Program 🎧	20–25 minutes	All levels, ELL
	—— Linking Past and Present Activity 19, TCR 📁	15–20 minutes	L2
	—— Time Line Activity 19, TCR 📁	10–15 minutes	L1

	ASSESS MENU		
	Evaluate		
	—— Reading Essentials and Study Guide 19-3, TCR 📁	25–35 minutes	L1, ELL
	—— Section Quiz 19-3, TCR 📁	10–15 minutes	All levels
	Reteach		
	—— Reteaching Activity, TWE, p. 603	10–15 minutes	L1
	Enrich		
	—— Enrich, TWE, p. 601	5–10 minutes	L1

	CLOSE MENU		
	—— Close, TWE, p. 603	5–10 minutes	L1

See Optional Resources menu on page viii.

Grade _____ Class(es) _____ Date _____ M Tu W Th F

Teacher's Name _____ Date _____

Culture: Romanticism and Realism   Section 4 *(pp. 605–609)*

LOCAL OBJECTIVES	TWE—Teacher Wraparound Edition TCR—Teacher Classroom Resources 📁 Blackline Master 🖳 Transparency 💿 CD-ROM 🎧 Audio Program 📼 Videocassette 🖱 Internet Resources

	OBJECTIVES		
	1. At the end of the eighteenth century, romanticism emerged as a reaction to the ideas of the Enlightenment.		
	2. The Industrial Revolution created a new interest in science and helped produce the realist movement.		

	FOCUS MENU	**SUGGESTED TIME RANGES**	**SUGGESTED LEVEL**
	—— Bellringer Skillbuilder Activity, TWE, p. 605; used with Daily Focus Skills Transparency or Blackline Master 19-4, TCR 🖳 📁	5–10 minutes	L1
	—— Guide to Reading, TWE, p. 605	10–15 minutes	All levels
	—— Vocabulary PuzzleMaker 💿	15–20 minutes	All levels

	TEACH MENU		
	Guided Practice		
	—— Connecting Across Time, TWE, p. 606	10–15 minutes	L2
	—— Writing Activity, TWE, p. 606	15–20 minutes	L1
	—— Cooperative Learning Activity, TWE, p. 606	30–35 minutes	L2, ELL
	—— Interdisciplinary Connections Activity, TWE, p. 607	30–35 minutes	L2
	—— Graphic Organizer Transparencies and Strategies 19, TCR 🖳 📁	20–25 minutes	All levels
	—— History Simulation 19, TCR 📁	30–35 minutes	All levels
	Independent Practice		
	—— Guided Reading Activity 19-4, TCR 📁	15–20 minutes	L1, ELL
	—— Audio Program 🎧	20–25 minutes	All levels, ELL

	ASSESS MENU		
	Evaluate		
	—— Reading Essentials and Study Guide 19-4, TCR 📁	25–35 minutes	L1, ELL
	—— Section Quiz 19-4, TCR 📁	25–30 minutes	All levels
	—— Chapter 19 Tests, TCR 📁		
	—— Interactive Tutor Self-Assessment CD-ROM, TCR 💿	20–30 minutes	All levels
	—— MindJogger Videoquiz, Chapter 19 📼	20–25 minutes	All levels
	—— History Online Self-Check Quiz 19 🖱	15–20 minutes	All levels
	Reteach		
	—— Reteaching Activity, TWE, p. 609	10–15 minutes	L1
	—— Reteaching Activity 19, TCR 📁	15–20 minutes	L1

	CLOSE MENU		
	—— Close, TWE, p. 609	10–15 minutes	L1

See Optional Resources menu on page viii.

The Growth of Industrial Prosperity Section 1 *(pp. 615–619)*

LOCAL OBJECTIVES	TWE—Teacher Wraparound Edition TCR—Teacher Classroom Resources 📁 Blackline Master 🔦 Transparency 💿 CD-ROM 🎧 Audio Program 📼 Videocassette ⬭ Internet Resources

OBJECTIVES

1. New sources of energy and consumer products transformed the standard of living for all social classes in many European countries.

2. Working-class leaders used Marx's ideas to form socialist parties and unions.

FOCUS MENU	SUGGESTED TIME RANGES	SUGGESTED LEVEL
—— Bellringer Skillbuilder Activity, TWE, p. 615; used with Daily Focus Skills Transparency or Blackline Master 20-1, TCR 🔦 📁	5–10 minutes	L1
—— Guide to Reading, TWE, p. 615	15–20 minutes	All levels
—— Vocabulary Activity 20, TCR 📁	10–15 minutes	All levels
—— Vocabulary PuzzleMaker 💿	15–20 minutes	All levels
—— History Online Chapter 20 Overview ⬭	10–15 minutes	L1

TEACH MENU

Guided Practice

—— Meeting Individual Needs, TWE, p. 616	15–20 minutes	L1
—— Cooperative Learning Activity, TWE, p. 617	25–30 minutes	L1
—— Critical Thinking Activity, TWE, p. 618	10–15 minutes	L2, L3
—— Graphic Organizer Transparencies and Strategies 20, TCR 🔦 📁	20–25 minutes	All levels
—— History Simulation 20, TCR 📁	30–35 minutes	All levels

Independent Practice

—— Guided Reading Activity 20-1, TCR 📁	15–20 minutes	All levels
—— Audio Program 🎧	15–20 minutes	All levels

TEACH MENU

Evaluate

—— Reading Essentials and Study Guide 20-1, TCR 📁	25–35 minutes	L1, ELL
—— Section Quiz 20-1, TCR 📁	10–15 minutes	All levels
—— Interactive Tutor Self-Assessment CD-ROM, TCR 💿	20–30 minutes	All levels
—— MindJogger Videoquiz, Chapter 20 📼	20–25 minutes	All levels

Reteach

—— Reteaching Activity, TWE, p. 619	10–15 minutes	L1

CLOSE MENU

—— Close, TWE, p. 619	10–15 minutes	L2

See Optional Resources menu on page viii.

The Emergence of Mass Society   Section 2 (pp. 621–628)

LOCAL OBJECTIVES	TWE—Teacher Wraparound Edition TCR—Teacher Classroom Resources Blackline Master Transparency CD-ROM Audio Program Videocassette Internet Resources

OBJECTIVES

1. A varied middle class in Victorian Britain believed in the principles of hard work and good conduct.

2. New opportunities for women and the working class improved their lives.

FOCUS MENU	SUGGESTED TIME RANGES	SUGGESTED LEVEL
——— Bellringer Skillbuilder Activity, TWE, p. 621; used with Daily Focus Skills Transparency or Blackline Master 20-2, TCR	5–10 minutes	L1
——— Guide to Reading, TWE, p. 621	15–20 minutes	All levels
——— Vocabulary PuzzleMaker	15–20 minutes	All levels

TEACH MENU

Guided Practice

——— Meeting Individual Needs, TWE, p. 622	25–30 minutes	L2
——— Charting Activity, TWE, p. 623	5–10 minutes	L1
——— Connecting Across Time, TWE, p. 624	15–20 minutes	L1
——— Cooperative Learning Activity, TWE, p. 624	25–30 minutes	L1
——— Connecting Across Time, TWE, p. 626	10–15 minutes	L1
——— Writing Activity, TWE, p. 627	20–25 minutes	L2
——— Graphic Organizer Transparencies and Strategies 20, TCR	20–25 minutes	All levels
——— Cooperative Learning Activity 20, TCR	20–25 minutes	All levels

Independent Practice

——— Guided Reading Activity 20-2, TCR	15–20 minutes	L1, ELL
——— Audio Program	20–25 minutes	All levels, ELL
——— Primary Source Reading 20, TCR	20–25 minutes	L2
——— Critical Thinking Skills Activity 20, TCR	15–20 minutes	L2

TEACH MENU

Evaluate

——— Reading Essentials and Study Guide 20-2, TCR	25–35 minutes	L1, ELL
——— Section Quiz 20-2, TCR	10–15 minutes	All levels
——— Interactive Tutor Self-Assessment CD-ROM, TCR	20–30 minutes	All levels

Reteach

——— Reteaching Activity, TWE, p. 628	10–15 minutes	L1

Enrich

——— Enrich, TWE, p. 625	10–15 minutes	L1
——— Enrich, TWE, p. 628	10–15 minutes	L2
——— Enrichment Activity 20, TCR	15–20 minutes	L2

CLOSE MENU

——— Close, TWE, p. 628	5–10 minutes	L1

See Optional Resources menu on page viii.

The National State and Democracy   Section 3 *(pp. 629–634)*

LOCAL OBJECTIVES	TWE—Teacher Wraparound Edition TCR—Teacher Classroom Resources 📁 Blackline Master 🖌 Transparency 💿 CD-ROM 🎧 Audio Program 📼 Videocassette 🖱⁵ Internet Resources
	OBJECTIVES **1.** The governments of western Europe were challenged by the development of new political parties and labor unions. **2.** International rivalries led to conflicts in the Balkans and to World War I.

		SUGGESTED TIME RANGES	**SUGGESTED LEVEL**
	FOCUS MENU		
	—— Bellringer Skillbuilder Activity, TWE, p. 629; used with Daily Focus Skills Transparency or Blackline Master 20-3, TCR 🖌 📁	5–10 minutes	L1
	—— Guide to Reading, TWE, p. 629	5–10 minutes	All levels
	—— Vocabulary PuzzleMaker 💿	15–20 minutes	All levels
	TEACH MENU **Guided Practice**		
	—— Critical Thinking, TWE, p. 630	10–15 minutes	L1
	—— Interdisciplinary Connections Activity, TWE, p. 630	10–15 minutes	L2
	—— Critical Thinking, TWE, p. 631	5–10 minutes	L1
	—— Meeting Individual Needs, TWE, p. 631	20–25 minutes	L2
	—— Connecting Across Time, TWE, p. 632	15–20 minutes	L2
	—— Graphic Organizer Transparencies and Strategies 20, TCR 🖌 📁	20–25 minutes	All levels
	Independent Practice		
	—— Guided Reading Activity 20-3, TCR 📁	15–20 minutes	L1, ELL
	—— Skills Reinforcement Activity 20, TCR 📁	15–20 minutes	All levels
	—— Audio Program 🎧	20–25 minutes	All levels, ELL
	—— Historical Significance Activity 20, TCR 📁	15–20 minutes	L2
	TEACH MENU **Evaluate**		
	—— Reading Essentials and Study Guide 20-3, TCR 📁	25–35 minutes	L1, ELL
	—— Section Quiz 20-3, TCR 📁	10–15 minutes	All levels
	—— Interactive Tutor Self-Assessment CD-ROM, TCR 💿	20–30 minutes	All levels
	—— Performance Assessment Activity 20, TCR 📁	15–20 minutes	L2
	Reteach		
	—— Reteaching Activity, TWE, p. 634	10–15 minutes	L2
	CLOSE MENU —— Close, TWE, p. 634	5–10 minutes	L1

See Optional Resources menu on page viii.

Toward the Modern Consciousness   Section 4 (pp. 636–641)

LOCAL OBJECTIVES	TWE—Teacher Wraparound Edition TCR—Teacher Classroom Resources 📁 Blackline Master 🔦 Transparency 💿 CD-ROM 🎧 Audio Program 📼 Videocassette 🖱 Internet Resources

OBJECTIVES

1. Innovative artistic movements during the late 1800s and early 1900s rejected traditional styles.

2. Extreme nationalism and racism led to an increase in anti-Semitism.

3. Developments in science changed how people saw themselves and their world.

FOCUS MENU	SUGGESTED TIME RANGES	SUGGESTED LEVEL
—— Bellringer Skillbuilder Activity, TWE, p. 636; used with Daily Focus Skills Transparency or Blackline Master 20-4, TCR 🔦 📁	5–10 minutes	L1
—— Guide to Reading, TWE, p. 636	10–15 minutes	All levels
—— Vocabulary PuzzleMaker 💿	15–20 minutes	All levels

TEACH MENU		
Guided Practice		
—— Meeting Individual Needs, TWE, p. 637	25–30 minutes	L1
—— Critical Thinking Activity, TWE, p. 638	30–35 minutes	L1
—— Critical Thinking, TWE, p. 639	5–10 minutes	L2
—— Interdisciplinary Connections Activity, TWE, p. 639	20–25 minutes	L3
—— History Online Student Web Activity 20 🖱		
—— Cooperative Learning Activity, TWE, p. 640	30–35 minutes	L1
—— Graphic Organizer Transparencies and Strategies 20, TCR 🔦 📁	20–25 minutes	All levels
Independent Practice		
—— Guided Reading Activity 20-4, TCR 📁	15–20 minutes	L1, ELL
—— Audio Program 🎧	20–25 minutes	All levels, ELL
—— Linking Past and Present Activity 20, TCR 📁	15–20 minutes	L3
—— Time Line Activity 20, TCR 📁	10–15 minutes	L2

TEACH MENU		
Evaluate		
—— Reading Essentials and Study Guide 20-4, TCR 📁	25–35 minutes	L1, ELL
—— Section Quiz 20-4, TCR 📁	25–30 minutes	All levels
—— Chapter 20 Tests, TCR 📁		
—— MindJogger Videoquiz, Chapter 20 📼	20–25 minutes	All levels
—— History Online Self-Check Quiz 20 🖱	15–20 minutes	All levels
Reteach		
—— Reteaching Activity, TWE, p. 641	20–25 minutes	L1
—— Reteaching Activity 20, TCR 📁	15–20 minutes	L1
Enrich		
—— Enrich, TWE, p. 640	5–10 minutes	L2

CLOSE MENU		
—— Close, TWE, p. 641	15–20 minutes	L1

See Optional Resources menu on page viii.

Colonial Rule in Southeast Asia   Section 1 (pp. 647–652)

LOCAL OBJECTIVES	TWE—Teacher Wraparound Edition TCR—Teacher Classroom Resources 📁 Blackline Master 🖌 Transparency 💿 CD-ROM 🎧 Audio Program 📼 Videocassette 🖱 Internet Resources		
	OBJECTIVES **1.** Through the "new imperialism," Westerners sought to control vast territories. **2.** Colonial export policies exploited native populations and opened up markets for European manufactured goods.		
	FOCUS MENU	**SUGGESTED TIME RANGES**	**SUGGESTED LEVEL**
	—— Bellringer Skillbuilder Activity, TWE, p. 647; used with Daily Focus Skills Transparency or Blackline Master 21-1, TCR 🖌 📁	5–10 minutes	L1
	—— Guide to Reading, TWE, p. 647	15–20 minutes	All levels
	—— Vocabulary Activity 21, TCR 📁	10–15 minutes	All levels
	—— Vocabulary PuzzleMaker 💿	15–20 minutes	All levels
	—— History Online Chapter 21 Overview 🖱	10–15 minutes	L1
	TEACH MENU **Guided Practice**		
	—— Critical Thinking Activity, TWE, p. 648	5–10 minutes	L2
	—— Interdisciplinary Connections Activity, TWE, p. 649	10–15 minutes	L1
	—— Writing Activity, TWE, p. 650	15–20 minutes	L1
	—— Critical Thinking, TWE, p. 650	10–15 minutes	L2
	—— Writing Activity, TWE, p. 651	20–25 minutes	L1
	—— Critical Thinking, TWE, p. 651	5–10 minutes	L1, ELL
	—— Interdisciplinary Connections Activity, TWE, p. 651	25–30 minutes	L2
	—— Graphic Organizer Transparencies and Strategies 21, TCR 🖌 📁	20–25 minutes	All levels
	Independent Practice		
	—— Guided Reading Activity 21-1, TCR 📁	15–20 minutes	All levels
	—— Audio Program 🎧	15–20 minutes	All levels
	—— Historical Significance Activity 21, TCR 📁	10–15 minutes	L2
	ASSESS MENU **Evaluate**		
	—— Reading Essentials and Study Guide 21-1, TCR 📁	25–35 minutes	L1, ELL
	—— Section Quiz 21-1, TCR 📁	10–15 minutes	All levels
	—— Interactive Tutor Self-Assessment CD-ROM, TCR 💿	20–30 minutes	All levels
	—— MindJogger Videoquiz, Chapter 21 📼	20–25 minutes	All levels
	Reteach —— Reteaching Activity, TWE, p. 652	5–10 minutes	L1
	Enrich —— Enrich, TWE, p. 649	15–20 minutes	L1, ELL
	CLOSE MENU —— Close, TWE, p. 652	5–10 minutes	L1

See Optional Resources menu on page viii.

Empire Building in Africa

Section 2 (pp. 654–660)

LOCAL OBJECTIVES	TWE—Teacher Wraparound Edition 📁 Blackline Master ✋ Transparency 🎧 Audio Program 📼 Videocassette	TCR—Teacher Classroom Resources 💿 CD-ROM 🔗 Internet Resources

OBJECTIVES

1. Great Britain, France, Germany, Belgium, and Portugal placed virtually all of Africa under European rule.
2. Native peoples sought an end to colonial rule.

FOCUS MENU	SUGGESTED TIME RANGES	SUGGESTED LEVEL
—— Bellringer Skillbuilder Activity, TWE, p. 654; used with Daily Focus Skills Transparency or Blackline Master 21-2, TCR ✋ 📁	5–10 minutes	L1
—— Guide to Reading, TWE, p. 654	15–20 minutes	All levels
—— Vocabulary PuzzleMaker 💿	15–20 minutes	All levels

TEACH MENU

Guided Practice

—— Critical Thinking Activity, TWE, p. 655	10–15 minutes	L2
—— Critical Thinking, TWE, p. 656	15–20 minutes	L1
—— Charting Activity, TWE, p. 656	15–20 minutes	L1, ELL
—— Writing Activity, TWE, p. 656	15–20 minutes	L2
—— Cooperative Learning Activity, TWE, p. 656	30–35 minutes	L2
—— Interdisciplinary Connections Activity, TWE, p. 657	10–15 minutes	L2
—— Interdisciplinary Connections Activity, TWE, p. 659	10–15 minutes	L2
—— Graphic Organizer Transparencies and Strategies 21, TCR ✋ 📁	20–25 minutes	All levels
—— Cooperative Learning Activity 21, TCR 📁	20–25 minutes	All levels

Independent Practice

—— Guided Reading Activity 21-2, TCR 📁	15–20 minutes	L1, ELL
—— Skills Reinforcement Activity 21, TCR 📁	15–20 minutes	All levels
—— Audio Program 🎧	20–25 minutes	All levels, ELL
—— Critical Thinking Skills Activity 21, TCR 📁	15–20 minutes	L1

ASSESS MENU

Evaluate

—— Reading Essentials and Study Guide 21-2, TCR 📁	25–35 minutes	L1, ELL
—— Section Quiz 21-2, TCR 📁	10–15 minutes	All levels
—— Interactive Tutor Self-Assessment CD-ROM, TCR 💿	20–30 minutes	All levels

Reteach

—— Reteaching Activity, TWE, p. 660	5–10 minutes	L2

Enrich

—— Enrich, TWE, p. 658	15–20 minutes	L2

CLOSE MENU

—— Close, TWE, p. 660	5–10 minutes	L1

See Optional Resources menu on page viii.

British Rule in India Section 3 *(pp. 666–670)*

LOCAL OBJECTIVES	TWE—Teacher Wraparound Edition TCR—Teacher Classroom Resources 📁 Blackline Master 🖐 Transparency 💿 CD-ROM 🎧 Audio Program 📼 Videocassette 💾 Internet Resources

	OBJECTIVES
	1. British rule brought stability to India but destroyed native industries and degraded Indians.
	2. Mohandas Gandhi advocated nonviolent resistance to gain Indian independence from Great Britain.

	FOCUS MENU	**SUGGESTED TIME RANGES**	**SUGGESTED LEVEL**
	—— Bellringer Skillbuilder Activity, TWE, p. 666; used with Daily Focus Skills Transparency or Blackline Master 21-3, TCR 🖐 📁	5–10 minutes	L1
	—— Guide to Reading, TWE, p. 666	5–10 minutes	All levels
	—— Vocabulary PuzzleMaker 💿	15–20 minutes	All levels

	TEACH MENU		
	Guided Practice		
	—— Critical Thinking Activity, TWE, p. 667	10–15 minutes	L2
	—— Charting Activity, TWE, p. 668	5–10 minutes	L2
	—— Interdisciplinary Connections Activity, TWE, p. 668	5–10 minutes	L1
	—— Connecting Across Time, TWE, p. 669	15–20 minutes	L2
	—— Graphic Organizer Transparencies and Strategies 21, TCR 🖐 📁	20–25 minutes	All levels
	Independent Practice		
	—— Guided Reading Activity 21-3, TCR 📁	15–20 minutes	L1, ELL
	—— Audio Program 🎧	20–25 minutes	All levels, ELL
	—— Primary Source Reading 21, TCR 📁	20–25 minutes	L2

	ASSESS MENU		
	Evaluate		
	—— Reading Essentials and Study Guide 21-3, TCR 📁	25–35 minutes	L1, ELL
	—— Section Quiz 21-3, TCR 📁	10–15 minutes	All levels
	—— Interactive Tutor Self-Assessment CD-ROM, TCR 💿	15–20 minutes	L2
	Reteach		
	—— Reteaching Activity, TWE, p. 670	15–20 minutes	L1
	Enrich		
	—— Enrich, TWE, p. 667	10–15 minutes	L1
	—— Enrich, TWE, p. 670	5–10 minutes	L2
	—— Enrichment Activity 21, TCR 📁	10–15 minutes	L3

	CLOSE MENU		
	—— Close, TWE, p. 670	5–10 minutes	L1

See Optional Resources menu on page viii.

Nation Building in Latin America   Section 4 *(pp. 671–677)*

LOCAL OBJECTIVES	TWE—Teacher Wraparound Edition TCR—Teacher Classroom Resources 📁 Blackline Master 🕹 Transparency 💿 CD-ROM 🎧 Audio Program 📼 Videocassette ⌇ Internet Resources

OBJECTIVES

1. Latin American countries served as a source of raw materials for Europe and the United States.

2. Because land remained the basis of wealth and power, landed elites dominated Latin American countries.

		SUGGESTED TIME RANGES	SUGGESTED LEVEL
FOCUS MENU			
——	Bellringer Skillbuilder Activity, TWE, p. 671; used with Daily Focus Skills Transparency or Blackline Master 21-4, TCR 🕹 📁	5–10 minutes	L1
——	Guide to Reading, TWE, p. 671	10–15 minutes	All levels
——	Vocabulary PuzzleMaker 💿	15–20 minutes	All levels
TEACH MENU			
Guided Practice			
——	Charting Activity, TWE, p. 673	15–20 minutes	L3
——	Critical Thinking, TWE, p. 674	30–35 minutes	L2
——	Meeting Special Needs, TWE, p. 674	25–30 minutes	L1
——	Connecting Across Time, TWE, p. 675	10–15 minutes	L2
——	Interdisciplinary Connections Activity, TWE, p. 675	20–25 minutes	L2
——	History Online Student Web Activity 21 ⌇		
——	Graphic Organizer Transparencies and Strategies 21, TCR 🕹 📁	20–25 minutes	All levels
——	History Simulation 21, TCR 📁	30–35 minutes	All levels
Independent Practice			
——	Guided Reading Activity 21-4, TCR 📁	15–20 minutes	L1, ELL
——	Linking Past and Present Activity 21, TCR 📁	15–20 minutes	L2
——	Time Line Activity 21, TCR 📁	10–15 minutes	L2
ASSESS MENU			
Evaluate			
——	Reading Essentials and Study Guide 21-4, TCR 📁	25–35 minutes	L1, ELL
——	Section Quiz 21-4, TCR 📁	25–30 minutes	All levels
——	Chapter 21 Tests, TCR 📁		
——	History Online Self-Check Quiz 21 ⌇	15–20 minutes	All levels
——	Performance Assessment Activity 21, TCR 📁	15–20 minutes	All levels
Reteach			
——	Reteaching Activity, TWE, p. 677	5–10 minutes	L1
——	Reteaching Activity 21, TCR 📁	15–20 minutes	L1
Enrich			
——	Enrich, TWE, p. 673	5–10 minutes	L2
CLOSE MENU			
——	Close, TWE, p. 677	10–15 minutes	L2

See Optional Resources menu on page viii.

Grade _____ Class(es) _____ Date _____ M Tu W Th F

Teacher's Name _____ Date _____

The Decline of the Qing Dynasty Section 1 *(pp. 683–689)*

LOCAL OBJECTIVES	TWE—Teacher Wraparound Edition TCR—Teacher Classroom Resources

Blackline Master Transparency CD-ROM Audio Program Videocassette Internet Resources

OBJECTIVES
1. The Qing dynasty declined because of internal and external pressures.
2. Western nations increased their economic involvement with China.

FOCUS MENU	SUGGESTED TIME RANGES	SUGGESTED LEVEL
—— Bellringer Skillbuilder Activity, TWE, p. 683; used with Daily Focus Skills Transparency or Blackline Master 22-1, TCR	5–10 minutes	L1
—— Guide to Reading, TWE, p. 683	15–20 minutes	All levels
—— Vocabulary Activity 22, TCR	10–15 minutes	All levels
—— Vocabulary PuzzleMaker	15–20 minutes	All levels
—— History Online Chapter 22 Overview	10–15 minutes	L1

TEACH MENU
Guided Practice

—— Cooperative Learning Activity 22, TWE, p. 684	20–25 minutes	L2
—— History Online Student Web Activity 22		
—— Charting Activity, TWE, p. 686	15–20 minutes	L3
—— Writing Activity, TWE, p. 686	15–20 minutes	L1
—— Meeting Individual Needs, TWE, p. 686	15–20 minutes	L1
—— Critical Thinking, TWE, p. 687	10–15 minutes	L2
—— Graphic Organizer Transparencies and Strategies 22, TCR	20–25 minutes	All levels
—— History Simulation 22, TCR	30–35 minutes	All levels

Independent Practice

—— Guided Reading Activity 22-1, TCR	15–20 minutes	All levels
—— Skills Reinforcement Activity 22, TCR	15–20 minutes	All levels
—— Linking Past and Present Activity 22, TCR	15–20 minutes	L2
—— Primary Source Reading 22, TCR	15–20 minutes	L2
—— Historical Significance Activity 22, TCR	15–20 minutes	L3
—— Critical Thinking Skills Activity 22, TCR	10–15 minutes	L2

ASSESS MENU
Evaluate

—— Reading Essentials and Study Guide 22-1, TCR	25–35 minutes	L1, ELL
—— Section Quiz 22-1, TCR	10–15 minutes	All levels

Reteach

—— Reteaching Activity, TWE, p. 688	15–20 minutes	L1

Enrich

—— Enrich, TWE, p. 684	10–15 minutes	L2
—— Enrichment Activity 22, TCR	10–15 minutes	L1

CLOSE MENU

—— Close, TWE, p. 689	5–10 minutes	L2

See Optional Resources menu on page viii.

Revolution in China

Section 2 *(pp. 691–696)*

LOCAL OBJECTIVES	TWE—Teacher Wraparound Edition TCR—Teacher Classroom Resources 📁 Blackline Master 🕹 Transparency 💿 CD-ROM 🎧 Audio Program 📼 Videocassette Internet Resources

OBJECTIVES

1. Sun Yat-sen introduced reforms that led to a revolution in China.

2. The arrival of Westerners brought changes to the Chinese economy and culture.

FOCUS MENU	SUGGESTED TIME RANGES	SUGGESTED LEVEL
—— Bellringer Skillbuilder Activity, TWE, p. 691; used with Daily Focus Skills Transparency or Blackline Master 22-2, TCR 🕹 📁	5–10 minutes	L1
—— Guide to Reading, TWE, p. 691	15–20 minutes	All levels
—— Vocabulary PuzzleMaker 💿	15–20 minutes	All levels

TEACH MENU

Guided Practice

—— Critical Thinking, TWE, p. 692	5–10 minutes	L1
—— Critical Thinking Activity, TWE, p. 692	20–25 minutes	L2
—— Connecting Across Time, TWE, p. 694	15–20 minutes	L3
—— Cooperative Learning Activity, TWE, p. 694	30–35 minutes	L2
—— Meeting Individual Needs, TWE, p. 695	30–35 minutes	L2
—— Graphic Organizer Transparencies and Strategies 22, TCR 🕹 📁	20–25 minutes	All levels

Independent Practice

—— Guided Reading Activity 22-2, TCR 📁	15–20 minutes	L1, ELL
—— Audio Program 🎧	20–25 minutes	All levels, ELL

ASSESS MENU

Evaluate

—— Reading Essentials and Study Guide 22-2, TCR 📁	25–35 minutes	L1, ELL
—— Section Quiz 22-2, TCR 📁	10–15 minutes	All levels
—— Interactive Tutor Self-Assessment CD-ROM, TCR 💿	20–30 minutes	All levels

Reteach

—— Reteaching Activity, TWE, p. 695	10–15 minutes	L1

Enrich

—— Enrich, TWE, p. 692	20–25 minutes	L3

CLOSE MENU

—— Close, TWE, p. 696	10–15 minutes	L2

See Optional Resources menu on page viii.

Rise of Modern Japan
Section 3 *(pp. 697–704)*

LOCAL OBJECTIVES	TWE—Teacher Wraparound Edition TCR—Teacher Classroom Resources		

TWE—Teacher Wraparound Edition   TCR—Teacher Classroom Resources

📁 Blackline Master   ✋ Transparency   💿 CD-ROM

🎧 Audio Program   📼 Videocassette   🔗 Internet Resources

OBJECTIVES

1. Western intervention opened Japan, an island that had been isolated for 200 years, to trade.

2. The interaction between Japan and Western nations gave birth to a modern industrial society.

FOCUS MENU	SUGGESTED TIME RANGES	SUGGESTED LEVEL
—— Bellringer Skillbuilder Activity, TWE, p. 697; used with Daily Focus Skills Transparency or Blackline Master 22-3, TCR ✋ 📁	5–10 minutes	L1
—— Guide to Reading, TWE, p. 697	10–15 minutes	All levels
—— Vocabulary PuzzleMaker 💿	15–20 minutes	All levels

TEACH MENU
Guided Practice

	SUGGESTED TIME RANGES	SUGGESTED LEVEL
—— Critical Thinking Activity, TWE, p. 699	10–15 minutes	L2
—— Writing Activity, TWE, p. 700	15–20 minutes	L2
—— Critical Thinking Activity, TWE, p. 700	20–25 minutes	L2
—— Critical Thinking, TWE, p. 701	15–20 minutes	L2
—— Interdisciplinary Connections Activity, TWE, p. 701	10–15 minutes	L2
—— Meeting Individual Needs, TWE, p. 703	20–25 minutes	L2
—— Graphic Organizer Transparencies and Strategies 22, TCR ✋ 📁	20–25 minutes	All levels
—— Cooperative Learning Activity 22, TCR 📁	20–25 minutes	All levels

Independent Practice

—— Guided Reading Activity 22-3, TCR 📁	15–20 minutes	L1, ELL
—— Audio Program 🎧	20–25 minutes	All levels, ELL
—— Time Line Activity 22, TCR 📁	10–15 minutes	L1

ASSESS MENU
Evaluate

—— Reading Essentials and Study Guide 22-3, TCR 📁	25–35 minutes	L1, ELL
—— Section Quiz 22-3, TCR 📁	25–30 minutes	All levels
—— Chapter 22 Tests, TCR 📁		
—— Interactive Tutor Self-Assessment CD-ROM, TCR 💿	20–30 minutes	All levels
—— MindJogger Videoquiz, Chapter 22 📼	20–25 minutes	All levels
—— History Online Self-Check Quiz 22 🔗	15–20 minutes	All levels
—— Performance Assessment Activity 22, TCR 📁	15–20 minutes	All levels

Reteach

—— Reteaching Activity, TWE, p. 703	10–15 minutes	L1
—— Reteaching Activity 22, TCR 📁	15–20 minutes	L1

CLOSE MENU

—— Close, TWE, p. 704	5–10 minutes	L1

See Optional Resources menu on page viii.

Grade _____   Class(es) _____   Date _____   M Tu W Th F

Teacher's Name _____   Date _____

The Road to World War I
Section 1 *(pp. 717–720)*

LOCAL OBJECTIVES	TWE—Teacher Wraparound Edition 📁 Blackline Master 🔦 Transparency 🔊 Audio Program 📼 Videocassette	TCR—Teacher Classroom Resources 💿 CD-ROM 🖱 Internet Resources

OBJECTIVES

1. Militarism, nationalism, and a crisis in the Balkans led to World War I.
2. Serbia's determination to become a large, independent state angered Austria-Hungary and initiated hostilities.

FOCUS MENU	SUGGESTED TIME RANGES	SUGGESTED LEVEL
——— Bellringer Skillbuilder Activity, TWE, p. 717; used with Daily Focus Skills Transparency or Blackline Master 23-1, TCR 🔦 📁	5–10 minutes	L1
——— Guide to Reading, TWE, p. 717	15–20 minutes	All levels
——— Vocabulary Activity 23, TCR 📁	10–15 minutes	All levels
——— Vocabulary PuzzleMaker 💿	15–20 minutes	All levels
——— History Online Chapter 23 Overview 🖱	10–15 minutes	L1

TEACH MENU
Guided Practice

——— Critical Thinking Activity, TWE, p. 718	25–30 minutes	L2
——— Cooperative Learning Activity, TWE, p. 719	30–35 minutes	L2
——— Graphic Organizer Transparencies and Strategies 23, TCR 🔦 📁	20–25 minutes	All levels

Independent Practice

——— Guided Reading Activity 23-1, TCR 📁	15–20 minutes	All levels
——— Audio Program 🔊	15–20 minutes	All levels
——— Historical Significance Activity 23, TCR 📁	20–25 minutes	L2
——— Critical Thinking Skills Activity 23, TCR 📁	10–15 minutes	L1

ASSESS MENU
Evaluate

——— Reading Essentials and Study Guide 23-1, TCR 📁	25–35 minutes	L1, ELL
——— Section Quiz 23-1, TCR 📁	10–15 minutes	All levels
——— Interactive Tutor Self-Assessment CD-ROM, TCR 💿	20–30 minutes	All levels
——— MindJogger Videoquiz, Chapter 23 📼	20–25 minutes	All levels

Reteach

——— Reteaching Activity, TWE, p. 720	5–10 minutes	L1

CLOSE MENU

——— Close, TWE, p. 720	5–10 minutes	L1

See Optional Resources menu on page viii.

Grade _____ Class(es) _____ Date _____ M Tu W Th F

Teacher's Name _____ Date _____

The War   Section 2 *(pp. 721–727)*

LOCAL OBJECTIVES	TWE—Teacher Wraparound Edition	TCR—Teacher Classroom Resources		
	🗀 Blackline Master ✋ Transparency	🖫 CD-ROM		
	🎧 Audio Program 📼 Videocassette	🖛 Internet Resources		

OBJECTIVES

1. The stalemate at the Western Front led to new alliances, a widening of the war, and new weapons.

2. Governments expanded their powers, increased opportunities for women, and made use of propaganda.

FOCUS MENU	**SUGGESTED TIME RANGES**	**SUGGESTED LEVEL**
____ Bellringer Skillbuilder Activity, TWE, p. 721; used with Daily Focus Skills Transparency or Blackline Master 23-2, TCR ✋ 🗀	5–10 minutes	L1
____ Guide to Reading, TWE, p. 721	15–20 minutes	All levels
____ Vocabulary PuzzleMaker 🖫	15–20 minutes	All levels

TEACH MENU		
Guided Practice		
____ Critical Thinking, TWE, p. 722	5–10 minutes	L1
____ Meeting Individual Needs, TWE, p. 723	15–20 minutes	L1
____ Critical Thinking, TWE, p. 724	5–10 minutes	L3
____ Critical Thinking Activity, TWE, p. 724	30–35 minutes	L2, L3
____ Critical Thinking, TWE, p. 725	5–10 minutes	L2
____ Meeting Individual Needs, TWE, p. 725	15–20 minutes	L1, ELL
____ Interdisciplinary Connections Activity, TWE, p. 726	15–20 minutes	L2
____ Graphic Organizer Transparencies and Strategies 23, TCR ✋ 🗀	20–25 minutes	All levels
____ History Simulation 23, TCR 🗀	30–35 minutes	All levels
Independent Practice		
____ Guided Reading Activity 23-2, TCR 🗀	15–20 minutes	L1, ELL
____ Audio Program 🎧	20–25 minutes	All levels, ELL
____ Linking Past and Present Activity 23, TCR 🗀	15–20 minutes	L1

ASSESS MENU		
Evaluate		
____ Reading Essentials and Study Guide 23-2, TCR 🗀	25–35 minutes	L1, ELL
____ Section Quiz 23-2, TCR 🗀	10–15 minutes	All levels
____ Performance Assessment Activity 23, TCR 🗀	15–20 minutes	All levels
Reteach		
____ Reteaching Activity, TWE, p. 727	10–15 minutes	L1
Enrich		
____ Enrich, TWE, p. 727	10–15 minutes	L2
____ Enrichment Activity 23, TCR 🗀	15–20 minutes	L2

CLOSE MENU		
____ Close, TWE, p. 727	5–10 minutes	L1

See Optional Resources menu on page viii.

The Russian Revolution   Section 3 (pp. 732–737)

LOCAL OBJECTIVES	TWE—Teacher Wraparound Edition TCR—Teacher Classroom Resources
	📁 Blackline Master 🖊 Transparency 💿 CD-ROM
	🎧 Audio Program 📼 Videocassette 🖱 Internet Resources

OBJECTIVES

1. The czarist regime in Russia fell as a result of poor leadership.

2. The Bolsheviks under Lenin came to power.

3. Communist forces triumphed over anti-Communist forces.

FOCUS MENU	**SUGGESTED TIME RANGES**	**SUGGESTED LEVEL**
—— Bellringer Skillbuilder Activity, TWE, p. 732; used with Daily Focus Skills Transparency or Blackline Master 23-3, TCR 🖊 📁	5–10 minutes	L1
—— Guide to Reading, TWE, p. 732	5–10 minutes	All levels
—— Vocabulary PuzzleMaker 💿	15–20 minutes	All levels

TEACH MENU

Guided Practice

—— Critical Thinking, TWE, p. 733	10–15 minutes	L2
—— Cooperative Learning Activity, TWE, p. 733	30–35 minutes	L2
—— History Online Student Web Activity 23 🖱		
—— Critical Thinking, TWE, p. 735	10–15 minutes	L2
—— Writing Activity, TWE, p. 735	20–25 minutes	L3
—— Interdisciplinary Connections Activity, TWE, p. 735	20–25 minutes	L2
—— Writing Activity, TWE, p. 736	15–20 minutes	L3
—— Cooperative Learning Activity, TWE, p. 736	15–20 minutes	L2
—— Graphic Organizer Transparencies and Strategies 23, TCR 🖊 📁	20–25 minutes	All levels

Independent Practice

—— Guided Reading Activity 23-3, TCR 📁	15–20 minutes	L1, ELL
—— Audio Program 🎧	20–25 minutes	All levels, ELL
—— Primary Source Reading 23, TCR 📁	20–25 minutes	L2

ASSESS MENU

Evaluate

—— Reading Essentials and Study Guide 23-3, TCR 📁	25–35 minutes	L1, ELL
—— Section Quiz 23-3, TCR 📁	10–15 minutes	All levels
—— Interactive Tutor Self-Assessment CD-ROM, TCR 💿	15–20 minutes	L2

Reteach

—— Reteaching Activity, TWE, p. 737	15–20 minutes	L1

Enrich

—— Enrich, TWE, p. 737	15–20 minutes	L2

CLOSE MENU

—— Close, TWE, p. 737	5–10 minutes	L1

See Optional Resources menu on page viii.

End of the War

Section 4 (pp. 739–744)

LOCAL OBJECTIVES	TWE—Teacher Wraparound Edition TCR—Teacher Classroom Resources
	📁 Blackline Master 🖱 Transparency 💿 CD-ROM
	🎧 Audio Program 📼 Videocassette 🖱 Internet Resources

OBJECTIVES

1. Combined Allied forces stopped the German offensive.
2. Peace settlements brought political and territorial changes to Europe and created bitterness and resentment in several nations.

FOCUS MENU	SUGGESTED TIME RANGES	SUGGESTED LEVEL
—— Bellringer Skillbuilder Activity, TWE, p. 739; used with Daily Focus Skills Transparency or Blackline Master 23-4, TCR 🖱 📁	5–10 minutes	L1
—— Guide to Reading, TWE, p. 739	10–15 minutes	All levels
—— Vocabulary PuzzleMaker 💿	15–20 minutes	All levels

TEACH MENU		
Guided Practice		
—— Writing Activity, TWE, p. 740	15–20 minutes	L3
—— Cooperative Learning Activity, TWE, p. 740	30–35 minutes	L3
—— Critical Thinking, TWE, p. 742	10–15 minutes	L2
—— Meeting Special Needs, TWE, p. 742	20–25 minutes	L2
—— Connecting Across Time, TWE, p. 743	10–15 minutes	L2
—— Interdisciplinary Connections Activity, TWE, p. 743	15–20 minutes	L2
—— Graphic Organizer Transparencies and Strategies 23, TCR 🖱 📁	20–25 minutes	All levels
—— Cooperative Learning Activity 23, TCR 📁	20–25 minutes	All levels
Independent Practice		
—— Guided Reading Activity 23-4, TCR 📁	15–20 minutes	L1, ELL
—— Skills Reinforcement Activity 23, TCR 📁	15–20 minutes	All levels
—— Audio Program 🎧	20–25 minutes	All levels, ELL
—— Time Line Activity 23, TCR 📁	10–15 minutes	L2

ASSESS MENU		
Evaluate		
—— Reading Essentials and Study Guide 23-4, TCR 📁	25–35 minutes	L1, ELL
—— Section Quiz 23-4, TCR 📁	25–30 minutes	All levels
—— Chapter 23 Tests, TCR 📁		
—— History Online Self-Check Quiz 23 🖱	15–20 minutes	All levels
—— Performance Assessment Activity 23, TCR 📁	15–20 minutes	All levels
Reteach		
—— Reteaching Activity, TWE, p. 744	5–10 minutes	L1
—— Reteaching Activity 23, TCR 📁	15–20 minutes	L1
Enrich		
—— Enrich, TWE, p. 740	5–10 minutes	L2

CLOSE MENU		
—— Close, TWE, p. 744	5–10 minutes	L1

See Optional Resources menu on page viii.

The Futile Search for Stability   Section 1 *(pp. 751–756)*

LOCAL OBJECTIVES	TWE—Teacher Wraparound Edition TCR—Teacher Classroom Resources

TWE—Teacher Wraparound Edition   TCR—Teacher Classroom Resources
📁 Blackline Master   ⚒ Transparency   💿 CD-ROM
🎧 Audio Program   📼 Videocassette   💿 Internet Resources

OBJECTIVES
1. Peace and prosperity were short-lived after World War I.
2. After 1929, a global economic depression weakened the Western democracies.

FOCUS MENU

	SUGGESTED TIME RANGES	SUGGESTED LEVEL
____ Bellringer Skillbuilder Activity, TWE, p. 751; used with Daily Focus Skills Transparency or Blackline Master 24-1, TCR ⚒ 📁	5–10 minutes	L1
____ Guide to Reading, TWE, p. 751	15–20 minutes	All levels
____ Vocabulary Activity 24, TCR 📁	10–15 minutes	All levels
____ Vocabulary PuzzleMaker 💿	15–20 minutes	All levels
____ History Online Chapter 24 Overview 💿	10–15 minutes	L1

TEACH MENU
Guided Practice

____ Cooperative Learning Activity, TWE, p. 752	25–30 minutes	L2
____ Critical Thinking, TWE, p. 753	5–10 minutes	L2
____ Critical Thinking Activity, TWE, p. 753	15–20 minutes	L2
____ Connecting Across Time, TWE, p. 754	10–15 minutes	L2
____ Meeting Individual Needs, TWE, p. 755	20–25 minutes	L1, ELL
____ Connecting Across Time, TWE, p. 756	10–15 minutes	L2
____ Graphic Organizer Transparencies and Strategies 24, TCR ⚒ 📁	20–25 minutes	All levels

Independent Practice

____ Guided Reading Activity 24-1, TCR 📁	15–20 minutes	All levels
____ Skill Reinforcement Activity 24, TCR 📁	15–20 minutes	All levels
____ Audio Program 🎧	15–20 minutes	All levels
____ Linking Past and Present Activity 24, TCR 📁	15–20 minutes	L1
____ Historical Significance Activity 24, TCR 📁	15–20 minutes	L2

ASSESS MENU
Evaluate

____ Reading Essentials and Study Guide 24-1, TCR 📁	25–35 minutes	L1, ELL
____ Section Quiz 24-1, TCR 📁	10–15 minutes	All levels
____ MindJogger Videoquiz, Chapter 24 📼	20–25 minutes	All levels

Reteach

____ Reteaching Activity, TWE, p. 756	10–15 minutes	L1

Enrich

____ Enrich, TWE, p. 753	10–15 minutes	L2
____ Enrich, TWE, p. 754	15–20 minutes	L1, ELL
____ Enrichment Activity 24, TCR 📁	15–20 minutes	L2

CLOSE MENU

____ Close, TWE, p. 756	10–15 minutes	L2

See Optional Resources menu on page viii.

The Rise of Dictatorial Regimes   Section 2 (pp. 758–764)

LOCAL OBJECTIVES	TWE—Teacher Wraparound Edition TCR—Teacher Classroom Resources
	📁 Blackline Master 🖇 Transparency 💿 CD-ROM
	🎧 Audio Program 📼 Videocassette 🖱 Internet Resources

OBJECTIVES

1. Mussolini established a modern totalitarian state in Italy.

2. As leader of the Soviet Union, Stalin eliminated people who threatened his power.

FOCUS MENU	SUGGESTED TIME RANGES	SUGGESTED LEVEL
—— Bellringer Skillbuilder Activity, TWE, p. 758; used with Daily Focus Skills Transparency or Blackline Master 24-2, TCR 🖇 📁	5–10 minutes	L1
—— Guide to Reading, TWE, p. 758	15–20 minutes	All levels
—— Vocabulary PuzzleMaker 💿	15–20 minutes	All levels

TEACH MENU

Guided Practice

—— Critical Thinking Activity, TWE, p. 759	15–20 minutes	L2
—— Connecting Across Time, TWE, p. 760	10–15 minutes	L3
—— History Online Student Web Activity 24 🖱		
—— Critical Thinking, TWE, p. 760	5–10 minutes	L2
—— Cooperative Learning Activity, TWE, p. 760	30–35 minutes	L3
—— Connecting Across Time, TWE, p. 761	10–15 minutes	L3
—— Cooperative Learning Activity, TWE, p. 761	20–25 minutes	L2
—— Connecting Across Time, TWE, p. 762	5–10 minutes	L2
—— Writing Activity, TWE, p. 762	15–20 minutes	L3
—— Meeting Individual Needs, TWE, p. 762	15–20 minutes	L1, ELL
—— Critical Thinking, TWE, p. 764	5–10 minutes	L1
—— Graphic Organizer Transparencies and Strategies 24, TCR 🖇 📁	20–25 minutes	All levels

Independent Practice

—— Guided Reading Activity 24-2, TCR 📁	15–20 minutes	L1, ELL
—— Audio Program 🎧	20–25 minutes	All levels, ELL

ASSESS MENU

Evaluate

—— Reading Essentials and Study Guide 24-2, TCR 📁	25–35 minutes	L1, ELL
—— Section Quiz 24-2, TCR 📁	10–15 minutes	All levels
—— Interactive Tutor Self-Assessment CD-ROM, TCR 💿	20–30 minutes	All levels

Reteach

—— Reteaching Activity, TWE, p. 764	5–10 minutes	L1

CLOSE MENU

—— Close, TWE, p. 764	5–10 minutes	L2

See Optional Resources menu on page viii.

Grade _____ Class(es) _____ Date _____ M Tu W Th F

Teacher's Name _____ Date _____

REPRODUCIBLE LESSON PLAN 24–3

Hitler and Nazi Germany   Section 3 (pp. 766–771)

LOCAL OBJECTIVES	TWE—Teacher Wraparound Edition TCR—Teacher Classroom Resources 📁 Blackline Master 🖋 Transparency ⑨ CD-ROM 🎧 Audio Program 📼 Videocassette � Internet Resources

OBJECTIVES
1. Hitler and the Nazi Party established a totalitarian state in Germany.
2. Many Germans accepted the Nazi dictatorship while other Germans suffered greatly under Hitler's rule.

FOCUS MENU SUGGESTED TIME RANGES SUGGESTED LEVEL

—— Bellringer Skillbuilder Activity, TWE, p. 766; used with Daily Focus Skills Transparency or Blackline Master 24-3, TCR 🖋 📁 5–10 minutes L1
—— Guide to Reading, TWE, p. 766 5–10 minutes All levels
—— Vocabulary PuzzleMaker ⑨ 15–20 minutes All levels

TEACH MENU
Guided Practice
—— Meeting Individual Needs, TWE, p. 767 15–20 minutes L2
—— Charting Activity, TWE, p. 768 15–20 minutes L1, ELL
—— Connecting Across Time, TWE, p. 768 10–15 minutes L3
—— Critical Thinking, TWE, p. 768 10–15 minutes L2
—— Connecting Across Time, TWE, p. 769 10–15 minutes L3
—— Critical Thinking, TWE, p. 769 5–10 minutes L2
—— Critical Thinking Activity, TWE, p. 769 15–20 minutes L2
—— Critical Thinking Activity, TWE, p. 770 15–20 minutes L2
—— Graphic Organizer Transparencies and Strategies 24, TCR 🖋 📁 20–25 minutes All levels
Independent Practice
—— Guided Reading Activity 24-3, TCR 📁 15–20 minutes L1, ELL
—— Audio Program 🎧 20–25 minutes All levels, ELL
—— Primary Source Reading 24, TCR 📁 20–25 minutes L2
—— Critical Thinking Skills Activity 24, TCR 📁 10–15 minutes L2

ASSESS MENU
Evaluate
—— Reading Essentials and Study Guide 24-3, TCR 📁 25–35 minutes L1, ELL
—— Section Quiz 24-3, TCR 📁 10–15 minutes All levels
—— Interactive Tutor Self-Assessment CD-ROM, TCR ⑨ 15–20 minutes L2
Reteach
—— Reaching Activity, TWE, p. 771 10–15 minutes L2

CLOSE MENU
—— Close, TWE, p. 771 10–15 minutes L1, ELL

See Optional Resources menu on page viii.

Glencoe World History   **89**

Cultural and Intellectual Trends Section 4 *(pp. 772–775)*

LOCAL OBJECTIVES	TWE—Teacher Wraparound Edition	TCR—Teacher Classroom Resources
	🗀 Blackline Master ✊ Transparency	💿 CD-ROM
	🎧 Audio Program 📼 Videocassette	🖱 Internet Resources

OBJECTIVES

1. Radios and movies were popular forms of entertainment that were used to spread political messages.

2. New artistic and intellectual trends reflected the despair created by World War I and the Great Depression.

	FOCUS MENU	SUGGESTED TIME RANGES	SUGGESTED LEVEL
	——— Bellringer Skillbuilder Activity, TWE, p. 772; used with Daily Focus Skills Transparency or Blackline Master 24-4, TCR ✊ 🗀	5–10 minutes	L1
	——— Guide to Reading, TWE, p. 772	10–15 minutes	All levels
	——— Vocabulary PuzzleMaker 💿	15–20 minutes	All levels

TEACH MENU

Guided Practice

——— Interdisciplinary Connections Activity, TWE, p. 773	25–30 minutes	L2
——— Cooperative Learning Activity, TWE, p. 774	25–30 minutes	L1, ELL
——— Critical Thinking, TWE, p. 775	5–10 minutes	L3
——— Graphic Organizer Transparencies and Strategies 24, TCR ✊ 🗀	20–25 minutes	All levels
——— Cooperative Learning Activity 24, TCR 🗀	20–25 minutes	All levels
——— History Simulation 24, TCR 🗀	30–35 minutes	All levels

Independent Practice

——— Guided Reading Activity 24-4, TCR 🗀	15–20 minutes	L1, ELL
——— Audio Program 🎧	20–25 minutes	All levels, ELL
——— Time Line Activity 24, TCR 🗀	10–15 minutes	L1

ASSESS MENU

Evaluate

——— Reading Essentials and Study Guide 24-4, TCR 🗀	25–35 minutes	L1, ELL
——— Section Quiz 24-4, TCR 🗀	25–30 minutes	All levels
——— Chapter 24 Tests, TCR 🗀		
——— Interactive Tutor Self-Assessment CD-ROM, TCR 💿	20–30 minutes	All levels
——— MindJogger Videoquiz, Chapter 24 📼	20–25 minutes	All levels
——— History Online Self-Check Quiz 24 🖱	15–20 minutes	All levels
——— Performance Assessment Activity 24, TCR 🗀	20–25 minutes	All levels

Reteach

——— Reteaching Activity, TWE, p. 775	5–10 minutes	L1
——— Reteaching Activity 24, TCR 🗀	15–20 minutes	L1

CLOSE MENU

——— Close, TWE, p. 775	10–15 minutes	L2

See Optional Resources menu on page viii.

Nationalism in the Middle East
Section 1 *(pp. 781–785)*

LOCAL OBJECTIVES	TWE—Teacher Wraparound Edition	TCR—Teacher Classroom Resources
	📁 Blackline Master ⚒ Transparency	💿 CD-ROM
	🎧 Audio Program 📼 Videocassette	💾 Internet Resources

OBJECTIVES

1. Nationalism led to the creation of the modern states of Turkey, Iran, and Saudi Arabia.

2. The Balfour Declaration made Palestine a national Jewish homeland.

FOCUS MENU

	SUGGESTED TIME RANGES	SUGGESTED LEVEL
—— Bellringer Skillbuilder Activity, TWE, p. 781; used with Daily Focus Skills Transparency or Blackline Master 25-1, TCR ⚒ 📁	5–10 minutes	L1
—— Guide to Reading, TWE, p. 781	15–20 minutes	All levels
—— Vocabulary Activity 25, TCR 📁	10–15 minutes	All levels
—— Vocabulary PuzzleMaker 💿	15–20 minutes	All levels
—— History Online Chapter 25 Overview 💾	10–15 minutes	L1

TEACH MENU

Guided Practice

—— Critical Thinking, TWE, p. 782	5–10 minutes	L2
—— Critical Thinking Activity, TWE, p. 784	15–20 minutes	L2
—— Graphic Organizer Transparencies and Strategies 25, TCR ⚒ 📁	20–25 minutes	All levels

Independent Practice

—— Guided Reading Activity 25-1, TCR 📁	15–20 minutes	All levels
—— Audio Program 🎧	15–20 minutes	All levels
—— Linking Past and Present Activity 25, TCR 📁	15–20 minutes	L2
—— Primary Source Reading 25, TCR 📁	20–25 minutes	L2

ASSESS MENU

Evaluate

—— Reading Essentials and Study Guide 25-1, TCR 📁	25–35 minutes	L1, ELL
—— Section Quiz 25-1, TCR 📁	10–15 minutes	All levels
—— Interactive Tutor Self-Assessment CD-ROM, TCR 💿	20–30 minutes	All levels
—— MindJogger Videoquiz, Chapter 25 📼	20–25 minutes	All levels

Reteach

—— Reteaching Activity, TWE, p. 785	5–10 minutes	L1

Enrich

—— Enrich, TWE, p. 782	5–10 minutes	L1
—— Enrich, TWE, p. 784	15–20 minutes	L2

CLOSE MENU

—— Close, TWE, p. 785	10–15 minutes	L2

See Optional Resources menu on page viii.

Grade _____   Class(es) _____   Date _____   M Tu W Th F

Teacher's Name _____   Date _____

Nationalism in Africa and Asia   Section 2 *(pp. 786–791)*

LOCAL OBJECTIVES	TWE—Teacher Wraparound Edition TCR—Teacher Classroom Resources 📁 Blackline Master 🖋 Transparency 💿 CD-ROM 🎧 Audio Program 📼 Videocassette 🖱 Internet Resources

OBJECTIVES
1. Peoples in Africa and Asia began to agitate for independence.
2. Japan became an aggressive military state.
3. Soviet agents worked to spread communism around the world.

FOCUS MENU	SUGGESTED TIME RANGES	SUGGESTED LEVEL
____ Bellringer Skillbuilder Activity, TWE, p. 786; used with Daily Focus Skills Transparency or Blackline Master 25-2, TCR 🖋 📁	5–10 minutes	L1
____ Guide to Reading, TWE, p. 786	15–20 minutes	All levels
____ Vocabulary PuzzleMaker 💿	15–20 minutes	All levels

TEACH MENU
Guided Practice

____ Interdisciplinary Connections Activity, TWE, p. 787	10–15 minutes	L2
____ History Online Student Web Activity 25 🖱		
____ Cooperative Learning Activity, TWE, p. 789	30–35 minutes	L2
____ Critical Thinking, TWE, p. 790	10–15 minutes	L2
____ Critical Thinking Activity, TWE, p. 790	15–20 minutes	L3
____ Graphic Organizer Transparencies and Strategies 25, TCR 🖋 📁	20–25 minutes	All levels

Independent Practice

____ Guided Reading Activity 25-2, TCR 📁	15–20 minutes	L1, ELL
____ Audio Program 🎧	20–25 minutes	All levels, ELL

ASSESS MENU
Evaluate

____ Reading Essentials and Study Guide 25-2, TCR 📁	25–35 minutes	L1, ELL
____ Section Quiz 25-2, TCR 📁	10–15 minutes	All levels
____ Interactive Tutor Self-Assessment CD-ROM, TCR 💿	20–30 minutes	All levels
____ Performance Assessment Activity 25, TCR 📁	15–20 minutes	All levels

Reteach
| ____ Reteaching Activity, TWE, p. 791 | 5–10 minutes | L1 |

Enrich
| ____ Enrich, TWE, p. 789 | 5–10 minutes | L1 |
| ____ Enrichment Activity 25, TCR 📁 | 10–15 minutes | L2 |

CLOSE MENU
| ____ Close, TWE, p. 791 | 5–10 minutes | L1 |

See Optional Resources menu on page viii.

Revolutionary Chaos in China Section 3 (pp. 793–797)

LOCAL OBJECTIVES	TWE—Teacher Wraparound Edition TCR—Teacher Classroom Resources
	📁 Blackline Master 🔥 Transparency 💿 CD-ROM
	🎧 Audio Program 📼 Videocassette 💾 Internet Resources

	OBJECTIVES
	1. Internal tensions led Chiang Kai-shek to violently end the Communist-Nationalist alliance.
	2. Mao Zedong believed revolution in China would be led by peasants, not the urban working class.

	FOCUS MENU	**SUGGESTED TIME RANGES**	**SUGGESTED LEVEL**
	—— Bellringer Skillbuilder Activity, TWE, p. 793; used with Daily Focus Skills Transparency or Blackline Master 25-3, TCR 🔥 📁	5–10 minutes	L1
	—— Guide to Reading, TWE, p. 793	5–10 minutes	All levels
	—— Vocabulary PuzzleMaker 💿	15–20 minutes	All levels

	TEACH MENU		
	Guided Practice		
	—— Critical Thinking, TWE, p. 794	5–10 minutes	L2
	—— Cooperative Learning Activity, TWE, p. 794	15–20 minutes	L2
	—— Interdisciplinary Connections Activity, TWE, p. 796	25–30 minutes	L3
	—— Graphic Organizer Transparencies and Strategies 25, TCR 🔥 📁	20–25 minutes	All levels
	Independent Practice		
	—— Guided Reading Activity 25-3, TCR 📁	15–20 minutes	L1, ELL
	—— Skills Reinforcement Activity 25, TCR 📁	15–20 minutes	All levels
	—— Audio Program 🎧	20–25 minutes	All levels, ELL

	ASSESS MENU		
	Evaluate		
	—— Reading Essentials and Study Guide 25-3, TCR 📁	25–35 minutes	L1, ELL
	—— Section Quiz 25-3, TCR 📁	10–15 minutes	All levels
	—— Interactive Tutor Self-Assessment CD-ROM, TCR 💿	15–20 minutes	L2
	Reteach		
	—— Reteaching Activity, TWE, p. 797	10–15 minutes	L2
	Enrich		
	—— Enrich, TWE, p. 795	10–15 minutes	L2

	CLOSE MENU		
	—— Close, TWE, p. 797	5–10 minutes	L2

•ee Optional Resources menu on page viii.

Grade _____ Class(es) _____ Date _____ M Tu W Th F

Teacher's Name _____ Date _____

Nationalism in Latin America   Section 4 (pp. 799–803)

LOCAL OBJECTIVES	TWE—Teacher Wraparound Edition TCR—Teacher Classroom Resources 📁 Blackline Master ✋ Transparency 💿 CD-ROM 🎧 Audio Program 📼 Videocassette 🖱 Internet Resources

	OBJECTIVES **1.** Before the Great Depression, the United States was the foremost investor in Latin America. **2.** The Great Depression created instability in Latin America, which led to military coups and the creation of military dictatorships.

	FOCUS MENU	**SUGGESTED TIME RANGES**	**SUGGESTED LEVEL**
	—— Bellringer Skillbuilder Activity, TWE, p. 799; used with Daily Focus Skills Transparency or Blackline Master 25-4, TCR ✋ 📁	5–10 minutes	L1
	—— Guide to Reading, TWE, p. 799	10–15 minutes	All levels
	—— Vocabulary PuzzleMaker 💿	15–20 minutes	All levels

	TEACH MENU **Guided Practice**		
	—— Cooperative Learning Activity, TWE, p. 800	20–25 minutes	L2
	—— Writing Activity, TWE, p. 801	15–20 minutes	L2
	—— Meeting Individual Needs, TWE, p. 802	25–30 minutes	L1
	—— Graphic Organizer Transparencies and Strategies 25, TCR ✋ 📁	20–25 minutes	All levels
	—— Cooperative Learning Activity 25, TCR 📁	20–25 minutes	All levels
	—— History Simulation 25, TCR 📁	30–35 minutes	All levels
	Independent Practice		
	—— Guided Reading Activity 25-4, TCR 📁	15–20 minutes	L1, ELL
	—— Audio Program 🎧	20–25 minutes	All levels, ELL
	—— Historical Significance Activity 25, TCR 📁	15–20 minutes	L2
	—— Time Line Activity 25, TCR 📁	10–15 minutes	L2
	—— Critical Thinking Skills Activity 25, TCR 📁	15–20 minutes	L1

	ASSESS MENU **Evaluate**		
	—— Reading Essentials and Study Guide 25-4, TCR 📁	25–35 minutes	L1, ELL
	—— Section Quiz 25-4, TCR 📁	25–30 minutes	All levels
	—— Chapter 25 Tests, TCR 📁		
	—— MindJogger Videoquiz, Chapter 25 📼	20–25 minutes	All levels
	—— History Online Self-Check Quiz 25 🖱	15–20 minutes	All levels
	Reteach		
	—— Reteaching Activity, TWE, p. 803	5–10 minutes	L1
	—— Reteaching Activity 25, TCR 📁	15–20 minutes	L1
	Enrich		
	—— Enrich, TWE, p. 801	25–30 minutes	L2

	CLOSE MENU		
	—— Close, TWE, p. 803	10–15 minutes	L2

See Optional Resources menu on page viii.

Paths to War

Section 1 *(pp. 809–813)*

LOCAL OBJECTIVES	TWE—Teacher Wraparound Edition TCR—Teacher Classroom Resources 📁 Blackline Master ✋ Transparency 💿 CD-ROM 🎧 Audio Program 📼 Videocassette 🖱 Internet Resources

OBJECTIVES

1. Adolf Hitler's theory of Aryan racial domination laid the foundation for aggressive expansion outside of Germany.

2. The actions and ambitions of Japan and Germany paved the way for the outbreak of World War II.

FOCUS MENU	SUGGESTED TIME RANGES	SUGGESTED LEVEL
—— Bellringer Skillbuilder Activity, TWE, p. 809; used with Daily Focus Skills Transparency or Blackline Master 26-1, TCR ✋ 📁	5–10 minutes	L1
—— Guide to Reading, TWE, p. 809	15–20 minutes	All levels
—— Vocabulary Activity 26, TCR 📁	10–15 minutes	All levels
—— Vocabulary PuzzleMaker 💿	15–20 minutes	All levels
—— History Online Chapter 26 Overview 🖱	10–15 minutes	L1

TEACH MENU

Guided Practice

	SUGGESTED TIME RANGES	SUGGESTED LEVEL
—— Critical Thinking, TWE, p. 811	5–10 minutes	L2
—— Critical Thinking, TWE, p. 811	5–10 minutes	L2
—— Connecting Across Time, TWE, p. 811	10–15 minutes	L2
—— Cooperative Learning Activity, TWE, p. 811	25–30 minutes	L2
—— Critical Thinking, TWE, p. 812	5–10 minutes	L2
—— Critical Thinking Activity, TWE, p. 812	10–15 minutes	L2
—— Graphic Organizer Transparencies and Strategies 26, TCR ✋ 📁	20–25 minutes	All levels
—— History Simulation 26, TCR 📁	30–35 minutes	All levels

Independent Practice

—— Guided Reading Activity 26-1, TCR 📁	15–20 minutes	All levels
—— Audio Program 🎧	15–20 minutes	All levels

ASSESS MENU

Evaluate

—— Reading Essentials and Study Guide 26-1, TCR 📁	25–35 minutes	L1, ELL
—— Section Quiz 26-1, TCR 📁	10–15 minutes	All levels
—— Interactive Tutor Self-Assessment CD-ROM, TCR 💿	20–30 minutes	All levels
—— MindJogger Videoquiz, Chapter 26 📼	20–25 minutes	All levels

Reteach

—— Reteaching Activity, TWE, p. 813	10–15 minutes	L1

Enrich

—— Enrich, TWE, p. 810	10–15 minutes	L2

CLOSE MENU

—— Close, TWE, p. 813	10–15 minutes	L1

ee Optional Resources menu on page viii.

The Course of World War II   Section 2 *(pp. 814–822)*

LOCAL OBJECTIVES	TWE—Teacher Wraparound Edition TCR—Teacher Classroom Resources 📁 Blackline Master 🎮 Transparency 💿 CD-ROM 🎧 Audio Program 📼 Videocassette 🖱 Internet Resources

OBJECTIVES

1. The bombing of Pearl Harbor created a global war between the Allied and the Axis forces.

2. Allied perseverance and effective military operations, as well as Axis miscalculations, brought an end to the war.

FOCUS MENU	SUGGESTED TIME RANGES	SUGGESTED LEVEL
—— Bellringer Skillbuilder Activity, TWE, p. 814; used with Daily Focus Skills Transparency or Blackline Master 26-2, TCR 🎮 📁	5–10 minutes	L1
—— Guide to Reading, TWE, p. 814	15–20 minutes	All levels
—— Vocabulary PuzzleMaker 💿	15–20 minutes	All levels

TEACH MENU
Guided Practice

	SUGGESTED TIME RANGES	SUGGESTED LEVEL
—— Cooperative Learning Activity, TWE, p. 815	15–20 minutes	L2
—— Connecting Across Time, TWE, p. 816	10–15 minutes	L1
—— Critical Thinking, TWE, p. 816	10–15 minutes	L1
—— Meeting Individual Needs, TWE, p. 817	30–35 minutes	L1
—— Cooperative Learning Activity, TWE, p. 818	30–35 minutes	L3
—— Critical Thinking, TWE, p. 819	5–10 minutes	L2
—— Writing Activity, TWE, p. 819	15–20 minutes	L2
—— Meeting Individual Needs, TWE, p. 819	15–20 minutes	L1
—— Critical Thinking, TWE, p. 820	10–15 minutes	L2
—— Interdisciplinary Connections Activity, TWE, p. 820	10–15 minutes	L2
—— Critical Thinking, TWE, p. 822	20–25 minutes	L2
—— Graphic Organizer Transparencies and Strategies 26, TCR 🎮 📁	20–25 minutes	All levels

Independent Practice

	SUGGESTED TIME RANGES	SUGGESTED LEVEL
—— Guided Reading Activity 26-2, TCR 📁	15–20 minutes	L1, ELL
—— Audio Program 🎧	20–25 minutes	All levels, ELL

ASSESS MENU
Evaluate

	SUGGESTED TIME RANGES	SUGGESTED LEVEL
—— Reading Essentials and Study Guide 26-2, TCR 📁	25–35 minutes	L1, ELL
—— Section Quiz 26-2, TCR 📁	10–15 minutes	All levels

Reteach

—— Reteaching Activity, TWE, p. 822	5–10 minutes	L1

Enrich

—— Enrich, TWE, p. 817	15–20 minutes	L2
—— Enrichment Activity 26, TCR 📁	15–20 minutes	L2

CLOSE MENU

—— Close, TWE, p. 822	10–15 minutes	L1

See Optional Resources menu on page viii.

Grade _____   Class(es) _____   Date _____   M Tu W Th F

Teacher's Name _____   Date _____

The New Order and the Holocaust   Section 3 (pp. 824–829)

LOCAL OBJECTIVES	TWE—Teacher Wraparound Edition TCR—Teacher Classroom Resources 📁 Blackline Master ♟ Transparency 💿 CD-ROM 🎧 Audio Program 📼 Videocassette ⌐ Internet Resources

	OBJECTIVES **1.** Adolf Hitler's philosophy of Aryan superiority led to the Holocaust. **2.** The Japanese conquest of Southeast Asia forced millions of native peoples to labor for the Japanese war machine.		
	FOCUS MENU	**SUGGESTED TIME RANGES**	**SUGGESTED LEVEL**
	——— Bellringer Skillbuilder Activity, TWE, p. 824; used with Daily Focus Skills Transparency or Blackline Master 26-3, TCR ♟ 📁	5–10 minutes	L1
	——— Guide to Reading, TWE, p. 824	5–10 minutes	All levels
	——— Vocabulary PuzzleMaker 💿	15–20 minutes	All levels
	TEACH MENU **Guided Practice**		
	——— Critical Thinking, TWE, p. 825	5–10 minutes	L2
	——— Connecting Across Time, TWE, p. 825	5–10 minutes	L2
	——— Critical Thinking Activity, TWE, p. 825	25–30 minutes	L2, L3
	——— Cooperative Learning Activity, TWE, p. 826	30–35 minutes	L2
	——— History Online Student Web Activity 26 ⌐		
	——— Writing Activity, TWE, p. 827	10–15 minutes	L3
	——— Connecting Across Time, TWE, p. 827	10–15 minutes	L2
	——— Critical Thinking Activity, TWE, p. 827	20–25 minutes	L2
	——— Graphic Organizer Transparencies and Strategies 26, TCR ♟ 📁	20–25 minutes	All levels
	——— Cooperative Learning Activity 26, TCR 📁	20–25 minutes	All levels
	Independent Practice		
	——— Guided Reading Activity 26-3, TCR 📁	15–20 minutes	L1, ELL
	——— Audio Program 🎧	20–25 minutes	All levels, ELL
	——— Primary Source Reading 26, TCR 📁	20–25 minutes	L2
	——— Historical Significance Activity 26, TCR 📁	10–15 minutes	L2
	ASSESS MENU **Evaluate**		
	——— Reading Essentials and Study Guide 26-3, TCR 📁	25–35 minutes	L1, ELL
	——— Section Quiz 26-3, TCR 📁	10–15 minutes	All levels
	Reteach ——— Reteaching Activity, TWE, p. 829	5–10 minutes	L2
	Enrich ——— Enrich, TWE, p. 826	20–25 minutes	L2
	——— Enrich, TWE, p. 829	10–15 minutes	L1
	CLOSE MENU ——— Close, TWE, p. 829	5–10 minutes	L1

ee Optional Resources menu on page viii.

The Home Front and the Aftermath of the War

Section 4 *(pp. 830–836)*

LOCAL OBJECTIVES	TWE—Teacher Wraparound Edition TCR—Teacher Classroom Resources		
	📁 Blackline Master 🎚 Transparency 💿 CD-ROM		
	🎧 Audio Program 📼 Videocassette ➤ Internet Resources		

	OBJECTIVES		
	1. World War II left a lasting impression on civilian populations.		
	2. The end of the war created a new set of problems for the Allies as the West came into conflict with the Soviet Union.		

	FOCUS MENU	**SUGGESTED TIME RANGES**	**SUGGESTED LEVEL**
	—— Bellringer Skillbuilder Activity, TWE, p. 830; used with Daily Focus Skills Transparency or Blackline Master 26-4, TCR 🎚 📁	5–10 minutes	L1
	—— Guide to Reading, TWE, p. 830	10–15 minutes	All levels
	—— Vocabulary PuzzleMaker 💿	15–20 minutes	All levels
	TEACH MENU		
	Guided Practice		
	—— Cooperative Learning Activity, TWE, p. 832	25–30 minutes	L2
	—— Meeting Individual Needs, TWE, p. 833	15–20 minutes	L1
	—— Interdisciplinary Connections Activity, TWE, p. 834	25–30 minutes	L2
	—— Critical Thinking Activity, TWE, p. 835	15–20 minutes	L1
	—— Graphic Organizer Transparencies and Strategies 26, TCR 🎚 📁	20–25 minutes	All levels
	Independent Practice		
	—— Guided Reading Activity 26-4, TCR 📁	15–20 minutes	L1, ELL
	—— Audio Program 🎧	20–25 minutes	All levels, ELL
	—— Linking Past and Present Activity 26, TCR 📁	15–20 minutes	L2
	—— Time Line Activity 26, TCR 📁	10–15 minutes	L1
	ASSESS MENU		
	Evaluate		
	—— Reading Essentials and Study Guide 26-4, TCR 📁	25–35 minutes	L1, ELL
	—— Section Quiz 26-4, TCR 📁	25–30 minutes	All levels
	—— Chapter 26 Tests, TCR 📁		
	—— History Online Self-Check Quiz 26 ➤	15–20 minutes	All levels
	—— Performance Assessment Activity 26, TCR 📁	20–25 minutes	All levels
	Reteach		
	—— Reteaching Activity, TWE, p. 836	10–15 minutes	L1
	—— Reteaching Activity 26, TCR 📁	15–20 minutes	L1
	Enrich		
	—— Enrich, TWE, p. 833	5–10 minutes	L1
	—— Enrichment Activity 26, TCR 📁	15–20 minutes	L3
	CLOSE MENU		
	—— Close, TWE, p. 836	5–10 minutes	L1

See Optional Resources menu on page viii.

Development of the Cold War   Section 1 *(pp. 849–854)*

LOCAL OBJECTIVES	TWE—Teacher Wraparound Edition TCR—Teacher Classroom Resources
	📁 Blackline Master 🎚 Transparency 💿 CD-ROM
	🎧 Audio Program 📼 Videocassette 🖱 Internet Resources

OBJECTIVES

1. A period of conflict called the Cold War developed between the United States and the Soviet Union after 1945.
2. As the Cold War developed, European nations were forced to support one of the two major powers.

FOCUS MENU	SUGGESTED TIME RANGES	SUGGESTED LEVEL
—— Bellringer Skillbuilder Activity, TWE, p. 849; used with Daily Focus Skills Transparency or Blackline Master 27-1, TCR 🎚 📁	5–10 minutes	L1
—— Guide to Reading, TWE, p. 849	15–20 minutes	All levels
—— Vocabulary Activity 27, TCR 📁	10–15 minutes	All levels
—— Vocabulary PuzzleMaker 💿	15–20 minutes	All levels
—— History Online Chapter 27 Overview 🖱	10–15 minutes	L1

TEACH MENU
Guided Practice

—— Connecting Across Time, TWE, p. 851	10–15 minutes	L2
—— Cooperative Learning Activity, TWE, p. 851	30–35 minutes	L3
—— Connecting Across Time, TWE, p. 852	5–10 minutes	L2
—— Meeting Individual Needs, TWE, p. 852	15–20 minutes	L1, ELL
—— Critical Thinking Activity, TWE, p. 853	10–15 minutes	L2
—— Graphic Organizer Transparencies and Strategies 27, TCR 🎚 📁	20–25 minutes	All levels

Independent Practice

—— Guided Reading Activity 27-1, TCR 📁	15–20 minutes	All levels
—— Audio Program 🎧	15–20 minutes	All levels
—— Primary Source Reading 27, TCR 📁	20–25 minutes	L2
—— Historical Significance Activity 27, TCR 📁	15–20 minutes	L2

ASSESS MENU
Evaluate

—— Reading Essentials and Study Guide 27-1, TCR 📁	25–35 minutes	L1, ELL
—— Section Quiz 27-1, TCR 📁	10–15 minutes	All levels
—— Interactive Tutor Self-Assessment CD-ROM, TCR 💿	20–30 minutes	All levels
—— MindJogger Videoquiz, Chapter 27 📼	20–25 minutes	All levels

Reteach

—— Reteaching Activity, TWE, p. 853	10–15 minutes	L1, ELL

Enrich

—— Enrich, TWE, p. 852	5–10 minutes	L1
—— Enrichment Activity 27, TCR 📁	10–15 minutes	L2

CLOSE MENU

—— Close, TWE, p. 854	5–10 minutes	L1

See Optional Resources menu on page viii.

Grade _____ Class(es) _____ Date _____ M Tu W Th F

Teacher's Name _____ Date _____

The Soviet Union and Eastern Europe Section 2 (pp. 855–858)

LOCAL OBJECTIVES	TWE—Teacher Wraparound Edition TCR—Teacher Classroom Resources
	📁 Blackline Master 🔦 Transparency 💿 CD-ROM
	🎧 Audio Program 📼 Videocassette 🖱 Internet Resources

OBJECTIVES

1. As Soviet leader, Khrushchev initiated policies of de-Stalinization.

2. The Soviet Union faced revolts and protests in its attempt to gain and maintain control over Eastern Europe.

		SUGGESTED TIME RANGES	SUGGESTED LEVEL
FOCUS MENU			
____	Bellringer Skillbuilder Activity, TWE, p. 855; used with Daily Focus Skills Transparency or Blackline Master 27-2, TCR 🔦 📁	5–10 minutes	L1
____	Guide to Reading, TWE, p. 855	15–20 minutes	All levels
____	Vocabulary PuzzleMaker 💿	15–20 minutes	All levels
TEACH MENU			
Guided Practice			
____	Interdisciplinary Connections Activity, TWE, p. 857	15–20 minutes	L3
____	History Online Student Web Activity 27 🖱		
____	Graphic Organizer Transparencies and Strategies 27, TCR 🔦 📁	20–25 minutes	All levels
____	Cooperative Learning Activity 27, TCR 📁	20–25 minutes	All levels
____	History Simulation 27, TCR 📁	30–35 minutes	All levels
Independent Practice			
____	Guided Reading Activity 27-2, TCR 📁	15–20 minutes	L1, ELL
____	Skills Reinforcement Activity 27, TCR 📁	15–20 minutes	All levels
____	Audio Program 🎧	20–25 minutes	All levels, ELL
____	Linking Past and Present Activity 27, TCR 📁	15–20 minutes	L1
____	Time Line Activity 27, TCR 📁	10–15 minutes	L2
ASSESS MENU			
Evaluate			
____	Reading Essentials and Study Guide 27-2, TCR 📁	25–35 minutes	L1, ELL
____	Section Quiz 27-2, TCR 📁	10–15 minutes	All levels
____	Interactive Tutor Self-Assessment CD-ROM, TCR 💿	20–30 minutes	All levels
Reteach			
____	Reteaching Activity, TWE, p. 858	10–15 minutes	L1, ELL
Enrich			
____	Enrich, TWE, p. 857	15–20 minutes	L2
CLOSE MENU			
____	Close, TWE, p. 858	5–10 minutes	L1

See Optional Resources menu on page viii.

Western Europe and North America   Section 3 (pp. 860–868)

LOCAL OBJECTIVES	TWE—Teacher Wraparound Edition TCR—Teacher Classroom Resources
	📁 Blackline Master 🖐 Transparency 💿 CD-ROM
	🔊 Audio Program 📼 Videocassette 🖱 Internet Resources

	OBJECTIVES
	1. Postwar Western societies rebuilt their economies and communities.
	2. Shifting social structures in the West led to upheaval and change.

	FOCUS MENU	**SUGGESTED TIME RANGES**	**SUGGESTED LEVEL**
	—— Bellringer Skillbuilder Activity, TWE, p. 860; used with Daily Focus Skills Transparency or Blackline Master 27-3, TCR 🖐 📁	5–10 minutes	L1
	—— Guide to Reading, TWE, p. 860	10–15 minutes	All levels
	—— Vocabulary PuzzleMaker 💿	15–20 minutes	All levels

	TEACH MENU		
	Guided Practice		
	—— Connecting Across Time, TWE, p. 861	10–15 minutes	L2
	—— Writing Activity, TWE, p. 861	30–35 minutes	L2
	—— Interdisciplinary Connections Activity, TWE, p. 861	25–30 minutes	L2
	—— Cooperative Learning Activity, TWE, p. 863	30–35 minutes	L2
	—— Critical Thinking, TWE, p. 865	10–15 minutes	L1, ELL
	—— Interdisciplinary Connections Activity, TWE, p. 866	20–25 minutes	L2
	—— Critical Thinking, TWE, p. 867	15–20 minutes	L2
	—— Graphic Organizer Transparencies and Strategies 27, TCR 🖐 📁	20–25 minutes	All levels
	Independent Practice		
	—— Guided Reading Activity 27-3, TCR 📁	15–20 minutes	L1, ELL
	—— Audio Program 🔊	20–25 minutes	All levels, ELL
	—— Critical Thinking Skills Activity 27, TCR 📁	10–15 minutes	L2

	ASSESS MENU		
	Evaluate		
	—— Reading Essentials and Study Guide 27-3, TCR 📁	25–35 minutes	L1, ELL
	—— Section Quiz 27-3, TCR 📁	25–30 minutes	All levels
	—— Chapter 27 Tests, TCR 📁		
	—— Interactive Tutor Self-Assessment CD-ROM, TCR 💿	20–30 minutes	All levels
	—— MindJogger Videoquiz, Chapter 27 📼	20–25 minutes	All levels
	—— History Online Self-Check Quiz 27 🖱	15–20 minutes	All levels
	—— Performance Assessment Activity 27, TCR 📁	15–20 minutes	All levels
	Reteach		
	—— Reteaching Activity, TWE, p. 868	5–10 minutes	L1, ELL
	—— Reteaching Activity 27, TCR 📁	15–20 minutes	L1
	Enrich		
	—— Enrich, TWE, p. 866	5–10 minutes	L2

	CLOSE MENU		
	—— Close, TWE, p. 868	5–10 minutes	L1

See Optional Resources menu on page viii.

Decline of the Soviet Union   Section 1 (pp. 875–878)

LOCAL OBJECTIVES	TWE—Teacher Wraparound Edition TCR—Teacher Classroom Resources
	📁 Blackline Master 👆 Transparency 💿 CD-ROM 🎧 Audio Program 📼 Videocassette 🖱 Internet Resources

OBJECTIVES
1. The Cold War ended after leadership changed in the Soviet Union.
2. Gorbachev's policies contributed to the disintegration of the Soviet Union.
3. Conversion from a socialist to a free-market economy has created many problems in the former Soviet states.

FOCUS MENU	SUGGESTED TIME RANGES	SUGGESTED LEVEL
—— Bellringer Skillbuilder Activity, TWE, p. 875; used with Daily Focus Skills Transparency or Blackline Master 28-1, TCR 👆 📁	5–10 minutes	L1
—— Guide to Reading, TWE, p. 875	15–20 minutes	All levels
—— Vocabulary Activity 28, TCR 📁	10–15 minutes	All levels
—— Vocabulary PuzzleMaker 💿	15–20 minutes	All levels
—— History Online Chapter 28 Overview 🖱	10–15 minutes	L1

TEACH MENU		
Guided Practice		
—— Meeting Individual Needs, TWE, p. 876	10–15 minutes	L1
—— Writing Activity, TWE, p. 877	15–20 minutes	L2
—— Cooperative Learning Activity, TWE, p. 877	25–30 minutes	L2
—— Graphic Organizer Transparencies and Strategies 28, TCR 👆 📁	20–25 minutes	All levels
Independent Practice		
—— Guided Reading Activity 28-1, TCR 📁	15–20 minutes	All levels
—— Audio Program 🎧	15–20 minutes	All levels
—— Critical Thinking Skills Activity 28, TCR 📁	10–15 minutes	L2

ASSESS MENU		
Evaluate		
—— Reading Essentials and Study Guide 28-1, TCR 📁	25–35 minutes	L1, ELL
—— Section Quiz 28-1, TCR 📁	10–15 minutes	All levels
—— Interactive Tutor Self-Assessment CD-ROM, TCR 💿	20–30 minutes	All levels
—— MindJogger Videoquiz, Chapter 28 📼	20–25 minutes	All levels
Reteach		
—— Reteaching Activity, TWE, p. 878	5–10 minutes	L1
Enrich		
—— Enrich, TWE, p. 876	5–10 minutes	L2

CLOSE MENU		
—— Close, TWE, p. 878	5–10 minutes	L2

See Optional Resources menu on page viii.

Eastern Europe

Section 2 (pp. 879–882)

LOCAL OBJECTIVES	TWE—Teacher Wraparound Edition TCR—Teacher Classroom Resources 📁 Blackline Master 🔦 Transparency 💿 CD-ROM 🎧 Audio Program 📼 Videocassette 🖱️ Internet Resources

OBJECTIVES

1. Gorbachev's policy of not giving military support to Communist governments created the opportunity for revolution.
2. Massive demonstrations peacefully ended some Communist regimes, while violence ended others.

FOCUS MENU	SUGGESTED TIME RANGES	SUGGESTED LEVEL
—— Bellringer Skillbuilder Activity, TWE, p. 879; used with Daily Focus Skills Transparency or Blackline Master 28-2, TCR 🔦 📁	5–10 minutes	L1
—— Guide to Reading, TWE, p. 879	15–20 minutes	All levels
—— Vocabulary PuzzleMaker 💿	15–20 minutes	All levels

TEACH MENU

Guided Practice

	SUGGESTED TIME RANGES	SUGGESTED LEVEL
—— History Online Student Web Activity 28 🖱️		
—— Cooperative Learning Activity, TWE, p. 880	30–35 minutes	L2
—— Graphic Organizer Transparencies and Strategies 28, TCR 🔦 📁	20–25 minutes	All levels
—— History Simulation 28, TCR 📁	30–35 minutes	All levels

Independent Practice

—— Guided Reading Activity 28-2, TCR 📁	15–20 minutes	L1, ELL
—— Audio Program 🎧	20–25 minutes	All levels, ELL
—— Primary Source Reading 28, TCR 📁	20–25 minutes	L2

ASSESS MENU

Evaluate

—— Reading Essentials and Study Guide 28-2, TCR 📁	25–35 minutes	L1, ELL
—— Section Quiz 28-2, TCR 📁	10–15 minutes	All levels
—— Interactive Tutor Self-Assessment CD-ROM, TCR 💿	20–30 minutes	All levels

Reteach

—— Reteaching Activity, TWE, p. 882	15–20 minutes	L1, ELL

Enrich

—— Enrichment Activity 28, TCR 📁	15–20 minutes	L2

CLOSE MENU

—— Close, TWE, p. 882	10–15 minutes	L3

See Optional Resources menu on page viii.

Europe and North America Section 3 *(pp. 884–888)*

LOCAL OBJECTIVES	TWE—Teacher Wraparound Edition Blackline Master Transparency Audio Program Videocassette	TCR—Teacher Classroom Resources CD-ROM Internet Resources

OBJECTIVES

1. Western European nations moved to unite their economies after 1970.

2. Domestic problems arose in the United States, Great Britain, France, Germany, and Canada.

FOCUS MENU	SUGGESTED TIME RANGES	SUGGESTED LEVEL
—— Bellringer Skillbuilder Activity, TWE, p. 884; used with Daily Focus Skills Transparency or Blackline Master 28-3, TCR	5–10 minutes	L1
—— Guide to Reading, TWE, p. 884	5–10 minutes	All levels
—— Vocabulary PuzzleMaker	15–20 minutes	All levels

TEACH MENU

Guided Practice

—— Critical Thinking, TWE, p. 885	5–10 minutes	L2
—— Cooperative Learning Activity, TWE, p. 885	25–30 minutes	L2
—— Meeting Individual Needs, TWE, p. 886	20–25 minutes	L1, ELL
—— Cooperative Learning Activity, TWE, p. 887	30–35 minutes	L1
—— Graphic Organizer Transparencies and Strategies 28, TCR	20–25 minutes	All levels

Independent Practice

—— Guided Reading Activity 28-3, TCR	15–20 minutes	L1, ELL
—— Audio Program	20–25 minutes	All levels, ELL
—— Time Line Activity 28, TCR	10–15 minutes	L2

ASSESS MENU

Evaluate

—— Reading Essentials and Study Guide 28-3, TCR	25–35 minutes	L1, ELL
—— Section Quiz 28-3, TCR	10–15 minutes	All levels
—— Interactive Tutor Self-Assessment CD-ROM, TCR	15–20 minutes	L2
—— Performance Assessment Activity 28, TCR	15–20 minutes	All levels

Reteach

—— Reteaching Activity, TWE, p. 888	10–15 minutes	L2

Enrich

—— Enrich, TWE, p. 886	20–25 minutes	L2
—— Enrich, TWE, p. 887	10–15 minutes	L2

CLOSE MENU

—— Close, TWE, p. 888	5–10 minutes	L2

See Optional Resources menu on page viii.

Western Society and Culture

Section 4 (pp. 889–894)

LOCAL OBJECTIVES	TWE—Teacher Wraparound Edition Blackline Master Transparency Audio Program Videocassette	TCR—Teacher Classroom Resources CD-ROM Internet Resources

OBJECTIVES

1. Technological and scientific advances have created a global society.
2. Artistic trends reflect how the emerging global society has led to a blending of cultural forms and ideas.

FOCUS MENU	SUGGESTED TIME RANGES	SUGGESTED LEVEL
—— Bellringer Skillbuilder Activity, TWE, p. 889; used with Daily Focus Skills Transparency or Blackline Master 28-4, TCR	5–10 minutes	L1
—— Guide to Reading, TWE, p. 889	10–15 minutes	All levels
—— Vocabulary PuzzleMaker	15–20 minutes	All levels

TEACH MENU		
Guided Practice		
—— Critical Thinking, TWE, p. 890	15–20 minutes	L1
—— Writing Activity, TWE, p. 891	20–25 minutes	L2
—— Connecting Across Time, TWE, p. 892	15–20 minutes	L3
—— Critical Thinking Activity, TWE, p. 892	20–25 minutes	L2
—— Critical Thinking, TWE, p. 893	5–10 minutes	L2
—— Meeting Individual Needs, TWE, p. 893	15–20 minutes	L1
—— Graphic Organizer Transparencies and Strategies 28, TCR	20–25 minutes	All levels
—— Cooperative Learning Activity 28, TCR	20–25 minutes	All levels
Independent Practice		
—— Guided Reading Activity 28-4, TCR	15–20 minutes	L1, ELL
—— Skills Reinforcement Activity 28, TCR	15–20 minutes	All levels
—— Audio Program	20–25 minutes	All levels, ELL
—— Linking Past and Present Activity 28, TCR	15–20 minutes	L2
—— Historical Significance Activity 28, TCR	10–15 minutes	L1

ASSESS MENU		
Evaluate		
—— Reading Essentials and Study Guide 28-4, TCR	25–35 minutes	L1, ELL
—— Section Quiz 28-4, TCR	25–30 minutes	All levels
—— Chapter 28 Tests, TCR		
—— MindJogger Videoquiz, Chapter 28	20–25 minutes	All levels
—— History Online Self-Check Quiz 28	15–20 minutes	All levels
Reteach		
—— Reteaching Activity, TWE, p. 894	10–15 minutes	L1
—— Reteaching Activity 28, TCR	15–20 minutes	L1

CLOSE MENU		
—— Close, TWE, p. 894	10–15 minutes	L2

See Optional Resources menu on page viii.

General Trends in Latin America   Section 1 *(pp. 901–905)*

LOCAL OBJECTIVES	TWE—Teacher Wraparound Edition TCR—Teacher Classroom Resources 📁 Blackline Master 🔥 Transparency 💿 CD-ROM 🎧 Audio Program 📼 Videocassette ⌁ Internet Resources

OBJECTIVES

1. Exporting raw materials and importing manufactured goods has led to economic and political troubles for Latin American nations.

2. Many Latin American nations began to build democratic systems in the late 1980s.

FOCUS MENU	**SUGGESTED TIME RANGES**	**SUGGESTED LEVEL**
—— Bellringer Skillbuilder Activity, TWE, p. 901; used with Daily Focus Skills Transparency or Blackline Master 29-1, TCR 🔥 📁	5–10 minutes	L1
—— Guide to Reading, TWE, p. 901	15–20 minutes	All levels
—— Vocabulary Activity 29, TCR 📁	10–15 minutes	All levels
—— Vocabulary PuzzleMaker 💿	15–20 minutes	All levels
—— History Online Chapter 29 Overview ⌁	10–15 minutes	L1

TEACH MENU

Guided Practice

—— Critical Thinking, TWE, p. 902	10–15 minutes	L2
—— Interdisciplinary Connections Activity, TWE, p. 902	20–25 minutes	L2
—— Interdisciplinary Connections Activity, TWE, p. 903	15–20 minutes	L1
—— Graphic Organizer Transparencies and Strategies 29, TCR 🔥 📁	20–25 minutes	All levels

Independent Practice

—— Guided Reading Activity 29-1, TCR 📁	15–20 minutes	All levels
—— Audio Program 🎧	15–20 minutes	All levels

ASSESS MENU

Evaluate

—— Reading Essentials and Study Guide 29-1, TCR 📁	25–35 minutes	L1, ELL
—— Section Quiz 29-1, TCR 📁	10–15 minutes	All levels
—— Interactive Tutor Self-Assessment CD-ROM, TCR 💿	20–30 minutes	All levels
—— MindJogger Videoquiz, Chapter 29 📼	20–25 minutes	All levels

Reteach

—— Reteaching Activity, TWE, p. 905	10–15 minutes	L1

Enrich

—— Enrich, TWE, p. 902	10–15 minutes	L3

CLOSE MENU

—— Close, TWE, p. 905	15–20 minutes	L1

See Optional Resources menu on page viii.

Grade _____ Class(es) _____ Date _____ M Tu W Th F

Teacher's Name _____ Date _____

Mexico, Cuba, and Central America Section 2 (pp. 906–909)

LOCAL OBJECTIVES	TWE—Teacher Wraparound Edition TCR—Teacher Classroom Resources

Blackline Master   Transparency   CD-ROM

Audio Program   Videocassette   Internet Resources

OBJECTIVES

1. Mexico and Central America faced political and economic crises after World War II.

2. The United States feared the spread of communism in Central American countries, which led to active American involvement in the region.

FOCUS MENU	SUGGESTED TIME RANGES	SUGGESTED LEVEL
—— Bellringer Skillbuilder Activity, TWE, p. 906; used with Daily Focus Skills Transparency or Blackline Master 29-2, TCR	5–10 minutes	L1
—— Guide to Reading, TWE, p. 906	15–20 minutes	All levels
—— Vocabulary PuzzleMaker	15–20 minutes	All levels

TEACH MENU

Guided Practice

	SUGGESTED TIME RANGES	SUGGESTED LEVEL
—— History Online Student Web Activity 29		
—— Cooperative Learning Activity, TWE, p. 907	30–35 minutes	L3
—— Critical Thinking, TWE, p. 908	5–10 minutes	L1
—— Critical Thinking Activity, TWE, p. 908	20–25 minutes	L2
—— Graphic Organizer Transparencies and Strategies 29, TCR	20–25 minutes	All levels
—— Cooperative Learning Activity 29, TCR	20–25 minutes	All levels

Independent Practice

—— Guided Reading Activity 29-2, TCR	15–20 minutes	L1, ELL
—— Audio Program	20–25 minutes	All levels, ELL
—— Linking Past and Present Activity 29, TCR	15–20 minutes	L2
—— Historical Significance Activity 29, TCR	15–20 minutes	L2
—— Critical Thinking Skills Activity 29, TCR	15–20 minutes	L2

ASSESS MENU

Evaluate

—— Reading Essentials and Study Guide 29-2, TCR	25–35 minutes	L1, ELL
—— Section Quiz 29-2, TCR	10–15 minutes	All levels
—— Interactive Tutor Self-Assessment CD-ROM, TCR	20–30 minutes	All levels
—— Performance Assessment Activity 29, TCR	20–25 minutes	All levels

Reteach

—— Reteaching Activity, TWE, p. 909	10–15 minutes	L1

Enrich

—— Enrichment Activity 29, TCR	10–15 minutes	L3

CLOSE MENU

—— Close, TWE, p. 909	5–10 minutes	L1

See Optional Resources menu on page viii.

The Nations of South America   Section 3 *(pp. 911–914)*

LOCAL OBJECTIVES	TWE—Teacher Wraparound Edition TCR—Teacher Classroom Resources 📁 Blackline Master ♟ Transparency 💿 CD-ROM 🎧 Audio Program 📼 Videocassette 🖱 Internet Resources

OBJECTIVES

1. South American nations have experienced economic, social, and political problems.

2. Democracy has advanced in South America since the late 1980s.

FOCUS MENU	SUGGESTED TIME RANGES	SUGGESTED LEVEL
____ Bellringer Skillbuilder Activity, TWE, p. 911; used with Daily Focus Skills Transparency or Blackline Master 29-3, TCR ♟ 📁	5–10 minutes	L1
____ Guide to Reading, TWE, p. 911	10–15 minutes	All levels
____ Vocabulary PuzzleMaker 💿	15–20 minutes	All levels

TEACH MENU

Guided Practice

____ Critical Thinking, TWE, p. 912	5–10 minutes	L2
____ Interdisciplinary Connections Activity, TWE, p. 913	10–15 minutes	L3
____ Critical Thinking, TWE, p. 914	5–10 minutes	L2
____ Graphic Organizer Transparencies and Strategies 29, TCR ♟ 📁	20–25 minutes	All levels
____ History Simulation 29, TCR 📁	30–35 minutes	All levels

Independent Practice

____ Guided Reading Activity 29-3, TCR 📁	15–20 minutes	L1, ELL
____ Skills Reinforcement Activity 29, TCR 📁	15–20 minutes	All levels
____ Audio Program 🎧	20–25 minutes	All levels, ELL
____ Primary Source Reading 29, TCR 📁	20–25 minutes	L3
____ Time Line Activity 29, TCR 📁	10–15 minutes	L1

ASSESS MENU

Evaluate

____ Reading Essentials and Study Guide 29-3, TCR 📁	25–35 minutes	L1, ELL
____ Section Quiz 29-3, TCR 📁	25–30 minutes	All levels
____ Chapter 29 Tests, TCR 📁		
____ Interactive Tutor Self-Assessment CD-ROM, TCR 💿	20–30 minutes	All levels
____ MindJogger Videoquiz, Chapter 29 📼	20–25 minutes	All levels
____ History Online Self-Check Quiz 29 🖱	15–20 minutes	All levels

Reteach

____ Reteaching Activity, TWE, p. 914	5–10 minutes	L1
____ Reteaching Activity 29, TCR 📁	15–20 minutes	L1

Enrich

____ Enrich, TWE, p. 866	5–10 minutes	L2

CLOSE MENU

____ Close, TWE, p. 914	5–10 minutes	L2

See Optional Resources menu on page viii.

Grade _____   Class(es) _____   Date _____   M Tu W Th F

Teacher's Name _____   Date _____

Independence in Africa

Section 1 (pp. 921–927)

LOCAL OBJECTIVES	TWE—Teacher Wraparound Edition TCR—Teacher Classroom Resources 📁 Blackline Master ✋ Transparency 💿 CD-ROM 🔊 Audio Program 📼 Videocassette ☞ Internet Resources

OBJECTIVES
1. People hoped that independence would bring democratic governments, but many African nations fell victim to military regimes and one-party states.
2. Culturally and economically, African nations struggled to resolve the tension between the modern and the traditional.

		SUGGESTED TIME RANGES	SUGGESTED LEVEL
FOCUS MENU			
——	Bellringer Skillbuilder Activity, TWE, p. 921; used with Daily Focus Skills Transparency or Blackline Master 30-1, TCR ✋ 📁	5–10 minutes	L1
——	Guide to Reading, TWE, p. 921	15–20 minutes	All levels
——	Vocabulary Activity 30, TCR 📁	10–15 minutes	All levels
——	Vocabulary PuzzleMaker 💿	15–20 minutes	All levels
——	History Online Chapter 30 Overview ☞	10–15 minutes	L1
TEACH MENU			
Guided Practice			
——	Cooperative Learning Activity, TWE, p. 922	25–30 minutes	L2
——	Writing Activity, TWE, p. 923	10–15 minutes	L2
——	Meeting Individual Needs, TWE, p. 923	15–20 minutes	L2
——	Connecting Across Time, TWE, p. 924	5–10 minutes	L1
——	Cooperative Learning Activity, TWE, p. 925	30–35 minutes	L3
——	History Online Student Web Activity 30 ☞		
——	Graphic Organizer Transparencies and Strategies 30, TCR ✋ 📁	15–20 minutes	All levels
——	History Simulation 30, TCR 📁	30–35 minutes	All levels
Independent Practice			
——	Guided Reading Activity 30-1, TCR 📁	15–20 minutes	L2, L3
——	Skills Reinforcement Activity 30, TCR 📁	15–20 minutes	All levels
——	Audio Program 🔊	30–35 minutes	All levels, ELL
——	Primary Source Reading 30, TCR 📁	20–25 minutes	L2
——	Critical Thinking Skills Activity 30, TCR 📁	15–20 minutes	L1
ASSESS MENU			
Evaluate			
——	Reading Essentials and Study Guide 30-1, TCR 📁	25–35 minutes	L1, ELL
——	Section Quiz 30-1, TCR 📁	10–15 minutes	All levels
Reteach			
——	Reteaching Activity, TWE, p. 927	10–15 minutes	L1
Enrich			
——	Enrich, TWE, p. 923	5–10 minutes	L2
CLOSE MENU			
——	Close, TWE, p. 927	15–20 minutes	L1

See Optional Resources menu on page viii.

Grade _____ Class(es) _____ Date _____ M Tu W Th F

Teacher's Name _____ Date _____

Conflict in the Middle East   Section 1 *(pp. 929–934)*

LOCAL OBJECTIVES	TWE—Teacher Wraparound Edition 📁 Blackline Master 🔨 Transparency 🔊 Audio Program 📼 Videocassette	TCR—Teacher Classroom Resources 💿 CD-ROM ➤ Internet Resources

	OBJECTIVES
	1. Instability in various parts of the Middle East has led to armed conflict and mediation attempts from countries outside the region.
	2. In many Middle Eastern countries, an Islamic revival has influenced political and social life.

	FOCUS MENU	**SUGGESTED TIME RANGES**	**SUGGESTED LEVEL**
	____ Bellringer Skillbuilder Activity, TWE, p. 929; used with Daily Focus Skills Transparency or Blackline Master 30-2, TCR 🔨 📁	5–10 minutes	L1
	____ Guide to Reading, TWE, p. 929	10–15 minutes	All levels
	____ Vocabulary PuzzleMaker 💿	15–20 minutes	All levels

	TEACH MENU		
	Guided Practice		
	____ Interdisciplinary Connections Activity, TWE, p. 930	15–20 minutes	L3
	____ Critical Thinking Activity, TWE, p. 931	25–30 minutes	L2
	____ Interdisciplinary Connections Activity, TWE, p. 932	15–20 minutes	L2
	____ Connecting Across Time, TWE, p. 933	15–20 minutes	L2
	____ Critical Thinking Activity, TWE, p. 933	15–20 minutes	L2
	____ Graphic Organizer Transparencies and Strategies 30, TCR 🔨 📁	20–25 minutes	All levels
	Independent Practice		
	____ Guided Reading Activity 30-2, TCR 📁	15–20 minutes	L1, ELL
	____ Linking Past and Present Activity 30, TCR 📁	15–20 minutes	L2
	____ Historical Significance Activity 30, TCR 📁	10–15 minutes	L2

	ASSESS MENU		
	Evaluate		
	____ Reading Essentials and Study Guide 30-2, TCR 📁	25–35 minutes	L1, ELL
	____ Section Quiz 30-2, TCR 📁	25–30 minutes	All levels
	____ Chapter 30 Tests, TCR 📁		
	____ Interactive Tutor Self-Assessment CD-ROM, TCR 💿	20–30 minutes	All levels
	____ MindJogger Videoquiz, Chapter 30 📼	20–25 minutes	All levels
	____ History Online Self-Check Quiz 30 ➤	15–20 minutes	All levels
	____ Performance Assessment Activity 30, TCR 📁	20–25 minutes	All levels
	Reteach		
	____ Reteaching Activity, TWE, p. 934	10–15 minutes	L1
	____ Reteaching Activity 30, TCR 📁	15–20 minutes	L1
	Enrich		
	____ Enrichment Activity 30, TCR 📁	10–15 minutes	L1

	CLOSE MENU		
	____ Close, TWE, p. 934	10–15 minutes	L1

See Optional Resources menu on page viii.

Grade _____ Class(es) _____ Date _____ M Tu W Th F

Teacher's Name _____ Date _____

Communist China

Section 1 *(pp. 941–946)*

LOCAL OBJECTIVES	TWE—Teacher Wraparound Edition TCR—Teacher Classroom Resources

📁 Blackline Master   🔨 Transparency   💿 CD-ROM

🎧 Audio Program   📼 Videocassette   � Internet Resources

OBJECTIVES

1. Mao Zedong established a socialist society in China.
2. After Mao's death, modified capitalist techniques were used to encourage growth in industry and farming.

FOCUS MENU

	SUGGESTED TIME RANGES	SUGGESTED LEVEL
—— Bellringer Skillbuilder Activity, TWE, p. 941; used with Daily Focus Skills Transparency or Blackline Master 31-1, TCR 🔨 📁	5–10 minutes	L1
—— Guide to Reading, TWE, p. 941	15–20 minutes	All levels
—— Vocabulary Activity 31, TCR 📁	10–15 minutes	All levels
—— Vocabulary PuzzleMaker 💿	15–20 minutes	All levels
—— History Online Chapter 31 Overview ➘	10–15 minutes	L1

TEACH MENU
Guided Practice

—— History Online Student Web Activity 31 ➘		
—— Critical Thinking, TWE, p. 943	10–15 minutes	L2
—— Cooperative Learning Activity, TWE, p. 943	30–35 minutes	L2
—— Meeting Individual Needs, TWE, p. 944	15–20 minutes	L2
—— Critical Thinking, TWE, p. 945	5–10 minutes	L2
—— Graphic Organizer Transparencies and Strategies 31, TCR 🔨 📁	20–25 minutes	All levels

Independent Practice

—— Guided Reading Activity 31-1, TCR 📁	15–20 minutes	All levels
—— Skill Reinforcement Activity 31, TCR 📁	15–20 minutes	All levels
—— Audio Program 🎧	15–20 minutes	All levels
—— Linking Past and Present Activity 31, TCR 📁	15–20 minutes	L1
—— Primary Source Reading 31, TCR 📁	15–20 minutes	L2

ASSESS MENU
Evaluate

—— Reading Essentials and Study Guide 31-1, TCR 📁	25–35 minutes	L1, ELL
—— Section Quiz 31-1, TCR 📁	10–15 minutes	All levels
—— Interactive Tutor Self-Assessment CD-ROM, TCR 💿	20–30 minutes	All levels
—— MindJogger Videoquiz, Chapter 31 📼	20–25 minutes	All levels

Reteach

—— Reteaching Activity, TWE, p. 946	15–20 minutes	L1, ELL

Enrich

—— Enrich, TWE, p. 944	10–15 minutes	L3

CLOSE MENU

—— Close, TWE, p. 946	10–15 minutes	L2

See Optional Resources menu on page viii.

Independent States in South and Southeast Asia

Section 2 *(pp. 952–956)*

LOCAL OBJECTIVES	TWE—Teacher Wraparound Edition 📁 Blackline Master 🎙 Transparency 🎧 Audio Program 📼 Videocassette	TCR—Teacher Classroom Resources 💿 CD-ROM 🖱 Internet Resources

OBJECTIVES

1. British India was divided into two states: India, mostly Hindu, and Pakistan, mostly Muslim.

2. Many of the newly independent states of Southeast Asia attempted to form democratic governments but often fell subject to military regimes.

FOCUS MENU	**SUGGESTED TIME RANGES**	**SUGGESTED LEVEL**
—— Bellringer Skillbuilder Activity, TWE, p. 952; used with Daily Focus Skills Transparency or Blackline Master 31-2, TCR 🎙 📁	5–10 minutes	L1
—— Guide to Reading, TWE, p. 952	15–20 minutes	All levels
—— Vocabulary PuzzleMaker 💿	15–20 minutes	All levels

TEACH MENU		
Guided Practice		
—— Critical Thinking, TWE, p. 954	15–20 minutes	L2
—— Meeting Individual Needs, TWE, p. 954	15–20 minutes	L2
—— Cooperative Learning Activity, TWE, p. 955	20–25 minutes	L1
—— Graphic Organizer Transparencies and Strategies 31, TCR 🎙 📁	20–25 minutes	All levels
Independent Practice		
—— Guided Reading Activity 31-2, TCR 📁	15–20 minutes	L1, ELL
—— Audio Program 🎧	20–25 minutes	All levels, ELL
—— Historical Significance Activity 31, TCR 📁	10–15 minutes	L2
—— Critical Thinking Skills Activity 31, TCR 📁	20–25 minutes	L3

ASSESS MENU		
Evaluate		
—— Reading Essentials and Study Guide 31-2, TCR 📁	25–35 minutes	L1, ELL
—— Section Quiz 31-2, TCR 📁	10–15 minutes	All levels
—— Interactive Tutor Self-Assessment CD-ROM, TCR 💿	20–30 minutes	All levels
Reteach		
—— Reteaching Activity, TWE, p. 956	5–10 minutes	L1
Enrich		
—— Enrichment Activity 31, TCR 📁	10–15 minutes	L1

CLOSE MENU		
—— Close, TWE, p. 956	10–15 minutes	L1

See Optional Resources menu on page viii.

Grade _____ Class(es) _____ Date _____ M Tu W Th F

Teacher's Name _____ Date _____

REPRODUCIBLE LESSON PLAN 31–3

Japan and the Pacific

Section 3 *(pp. 957–962)*

LOCAL OBJECTIVES	TWE—Teacher Wraparound Edition TCR—Teacher Classroom Resources 📁 Blackline Master 🖱 Transparency 💿 CD-ROM 🎧 Audio Program 📼 Videocassette 🖱 Internet Resources

OBJECTIVES

1. Japan and the "Asian tigers" have created successful industrial societies.

2. Although Australia and New Zealand have identified themselves culturally and politically with Europe, in recent years they have been drawing closer to their Asian neighbors.

FOCUS MENU

	SUGGESTED TIME RANGES	SUGGESTED LEVEL
—— Bellringer Skillbuilder Activity, TWE, p. 957; used with Daily Focus Skills Transparency or Blackline Master 31-3, TCR 🖱 📁	5–10 minutes	L1
—— Guide to Reading, TWE, p. 957	10–15 minutes	All levels
—— Vocabulary PuzzleMaker 💿	15–20 minutes	All levels

TEACH MENU

Guided Practice

—— Cooperative Learning Activity, TWE, p. 958	25–30 minutes	L3
—— Meeting Individual Needs, TWE, p. 959	20–25 minutes	L1, L2
—— Interdisciplinary Connections Activity, TWE, p. 960	15–20 minutes	L3
—— Critical Thinking Activity, TWE, p. 961	25–30 minutes	L2
—— Graphic Organizer Transparencies and Strategies 31, TCR 🖱 📁	20–25 minutes	All levels
—— Cooperative Learning Activity 31, TCR 📁	20–25 minutes	All levels
—— History Simulation 31, TCR 📁	30–35 minutes	All levels

Independent Practice

—— Guided Reading Activity 31-3, TCR 📁	15–20 minutes	L1, ELL
—— Audio Program 🎧	20–25 minutes	All levels, ELL
—— Time Line Activity 31, TCR 📁	10–15 minutes	L1

ASSESS MENU

Evaluate

—— Reading Essentials and Study Guide 31-3, TCR 📁	25–35 minutes	L1, ELL
—— Section Quiz 31-3, TCR 📁	25–30 minutes	All levels
—— Chapter 31 Tests, TCR 📁		
—— Interactive Tutor Self-Assessment CD-ROM, TCR 💿	20–30 minutes	All levels
—— History Online Self-Check Quiz 31 🖱	15–20 minutes	All levels
—— Performance Assessment Activity 31, TCR 📁	15–20 minutes	All levels

Reteach

—— Reteaching Activity, TWE, p. 962	5–10 minutes	L1
—— Reteaching Activity 31, TCR 📁	15–20 minutes	L1

Enrich

—— Enrich, TWE, p. 959	5–10 minutes	L2

CLOSE MENU

—— Close, TWE, p. 962	10–15 minutes	L2

See Optional Resources menu on page viii.

The Challenges of Our World   Section 1 *(pp. 969–973)*

LOCAL OBJECTIVES	TWE—Teacher Wraparound Edition TCR—Teacher Classroom Resources 📁 Blackline Master ♟ Transparency 💿 CD-ROM 🎧 Audio Program 📼 Videocassette 🖊 Internet Resources		
	OBJECTIVES **1.** The world faces environmental, social, economic, and political challenges. **2.** The benefits of the technological revolution must be balanced against its costs.		
	FOCUS MENU	**SUGGESTED TIME RANGES**	**SUGGESTED LEVEL**
	—— Bellringer Skillbuilder Activity, TWE, p. 969; used with Daily Focus Skills Transparency or Blackline Master 32-1, TCR ♟ 📁	5–10 minutes	L1
	—— Guide to Reading, TWE, p. 969	15–20 minutes	All levels
	—— Vocabulary Activity 32, TCR 📁	10–15 minutes	All levels
	—— Vocabulary PuzzleMaker 💿	15–20 minutes	All levels
	—— History Online Chapter 32 Overview 🖊	10–15 minutes	L1
	TEACH MENU **Guided Practice**		
	—— Connecting Across Time, TWE, p. 970	15–20 minutes	L2
	—— Cooperative Learning Activity, TWE, p. 970	30–35 minutes	L2
	—— Critical Thinking, TWE, p. 971	15–20 minutes	L2
	—— Cooperative Learning Activity, TWE, p. 971	15–20 minutes	L2
	—— Critical Thinking Activity, TWE, p. 972	20–25 minutes	L2
	—— Graphic Organizer Transparencies and Strategies 32, TCR ♟ 📁	15–20 minutes	All levels
	Independent Practice		
	—— Guided Reading Activity 32-1, TCR 📁	15–20 minutes	L2, L3
	—— Audio Program 🎧	30–35 minutes	All levels, ELL
	—— Linking Past and Present Activity 32, TCR 📁	15–20 minutes	L2
	ASSESS MENU **Evaluate**		
	—— Reading Essentials and Study Guide 32-1, TCR 📁	25–35 minutes	L1, ELL
	—— Section Quiz 32-1, TCR 📁	10–15 minutes	All levels
	—— Interactive Tutor Self-Assessment CD-ROM, TCR 💿	20–30 minutes	All levels
	—— MindJogger Videoquiz, Chapter 32 📼	20–25 minutes	All levels
	Reteach —— Reteaching Activity, TWE, p. 973	5–10 minutes	L1
	CLOSE MENU —— Close, TWE, p. 973	10–15 minutes	L1, ELL

See Optional Resources menu on page viii.

Grade _____ Class(es) _____ Date _____ M Tu W Th F

Teacher's Name _____ Date _____

Global Visions

Section 2 (pp. 974–976)

LOCAL OBJECTIVES	TWE—Teacher Wraparound Edition TCR—Teacher Classroom Resources Blackline Master Transparency CD-ROM Audio Program Videocassette Internet Resources

OBJECTIVES

1. Organizations have been established to respond to global challenges.

2. Citizens' groups and nongovernmental organizations have also formed to address global concerns.

		SUGGESTED TIME RANGES	SUGGESTED LEVEL
FOCUS MENU			
——	Bellringer Skillbuilder Activity, TWE, p. 974; used with Daily Focus Skills Transparency or Blackline Master 32-2, TCR	5–10 minutes	L1
——	Guide to Reading, TWE, p. 974	10–15 minutes	All levels
——	Vocabulary PuzzleMaker	15–20 minutes	All levels
TEACH MENU			
Guided Practice			
——	History Online Student Web Activity 32		
——	Critical Thinking Activity, TWE, p. 975	15–20 minutes	L3
——	Graphic Organizer Transparencies and Strategies 32, TCR	20–25 minutes	All levels
——	Cooperative Learning Activity 32, TCR	20–25 minutes	All levels
——	History Simulation 32, TCR	30–35 minutes	All levels
Independent Practice			
——	Guided Reading Activity 32-2, TCR	15–20 minutes	L1, ELL
——	Skills Reinforcement Activity 32, TCR	15–20 minutes	All levels
——	Audio Program	20–25 minutes	All levels, ELL
——	Primary Source Reading 32, TCR	15–20 minutes	L2
——	Historical Significance Activity 32, TCR	10–15 minutes	L2
——	Time Line Activity 32, TCR	10–15 minutes	L2
——	Critical Thinking Skills Activity 32, TCR	15–20 minutes	L2
ASSESS MENU			
Evaluate			
——	Reading Essentials and Study Guide 32-2, TCR	25–35 minutes	L1, ELL
——	Section Quiz 32-2, TCR	25–30 minutes	All levels
——	Chapter 32 Tests, TCR		
——	History Online Self-Check Quiz 30	15–20 minutes	All levels
——	Performance Assessment Activity 32, TCR	20–25 minutes	All levels
Reteach			
——	Reteaching Activity, TWE, p. 976	5–10 minutes	L2
——	Reteaching Activity 32, TCR	15–20 minutes	L1
Enrich			
——	Enrichment Activity 32, TCR	10–15 minutes	L1
CLOSE MENU			
——	Close, TWE, p. 976	10–15 minutes	L1

See Optional Resources menu on page viii.